Soprano Volume 4

THE SINGERS MUSICAL THEATRE ANTHOLOGY

A collection of songs from the musical stage, categorized by voice type. The selections are presented in their authentic settings, excerpted from the original vocal scores.

Compiled and Edited by Richard Walters

ISBN 1-4234-0023-2

HAL•LEONARD® CORPORATION

7777 W. BLUEMOUND RD. P.O. BOX 13819 MILWAUKEE, WI 53213

Visit Hal Leonard Online at
www.halleonard.com

Foreword

When I conceived and compiled the first volumes of *The Singer's Musical Theatre Anthology*, released in 1987, I couldn't have possibly imagined the day when I would be writing the foreword for Volume 4. Such a venture is made possible only by the lively and sustained interest of singing actors of all descriptions, be they students or professionals. As a researcher I can only present you with practical choices from existing theatre literature. Without the dedicated pursuit of that music by people such as you, dear reader, these collections would remain on a shelf, unopened.

Volume 4 allows inclusion of songs from shows opened since Volume 3 (released in 2000), as well as a continuing, deeper look into both classic and contemporary musical theatre repertory. As has been the case with each of the solo voice volumes in this series, songs are chosen with many types of talent in mind. All songs do not suit all singers. It is good and natural for any performer to stretch as far as possible, attempting diverse material. But it is also very important ultimately to know what you do well. That is an individual answer, based on your voice, your temperament and your look. This collection has enough variety of songs that any interested performer should be able to find several viable choices.

You will come up with a more individual interpretation, conjured from the ground up in the manner that all the best actors work, if you learn a song on your own, building it into your unique singing voice, *without* imitating a recorded performance. Particularly try to avoid copying especially famous renditions of a song, because you can probably only suffer in the comparison. Would you learn a role from Shakespeare, Shaw or Edward Albee solely by mimicking a recording, film or video/DVD of it? Your answer had better be *of course not!* The same needs to be true of theatre music. After you know the notes and lyrics very well, study the character's stated and unstated motivations and thoughts to come up with your own performance. Explore your own ideas about musical and vocal phrasing to express the character's emotions. In other words, make a song your own, and no one can take it away from you. It's yours for life.

Original keys are used exclusively in this edition. Sometimes these reflect the composer's musical/vocal concept, and sometimes they are merely the keys best suited to the original performers. Still, they give a singer a very good idea of the desired vocal timbre for a song as presented in its authentic theatre context. There are general vocal guidelines for voice types in theatre music, but these are not in stone. A soprano with a good belt will be able to sing songs from the soprano volumes as well as the mezzo-soprano/belter volumes. Belters may decide to work on their "head voice" in soprano songs. Men who have voices that lie between tenor and baritone, commonly called "baritenors" (a common range in contemporary musical theatre), may find songs in both the tenor and baritone/bass volumes.

In my foreword for Volume 3 of *The Singer's Musical Theatre Anthology*, written in 2000, I stated that the movie musical was dead. What a difference five years makes! The genre appears to be gaining a little steam at this writing, evidence of the continued relevance of musical theatre to a wider audience.

The books comprising Volume 4 of this series would not have been possible without the enthusiastic help of Brian Dean as assistant editor, and I thank him heartily.

All the selections from all volumes of this series, including duets, total nearly 700 songs. A marathon performance of all the songs in all volumes of *The Singer's Musical Theatre Anthology* would take more than 40 hours. What fun that would be!

Richard Walters,
December, 2005

THE SINGER'S MUSICAL THEATRE ANTHOLOGY

Soprano Volume 4

Contents

BEAUTY AND THE BEAST
14   Home

THE BOY FRIEND
20   I Could Be Happy with You
25   It's Nicer in Nice

BYE BYE BIRDIE
30   How Lovely to Be a Woman
38   One Boy

CINDERELLA
46   A Lovely Night

A DATE WITH JUDY (film)
41   It's a Most Unusual Day

A DAY IN HOLLYWOOD/
A NIGHT IN THE UKRAINE
50   Nelson

DRAT! THE CAT!
55   I Like Him

FANNY
58   I Have to Tell You

FLORA, THE RED MENACE
66   A Quiet Thing

A FUNNY THING HAPPENED
ON THE WAY TO THE FORUM
61   Lovely

INTO THE WOODS
70   On the Steps of the Palace
77   Children Will Listen

THE KING AND I
82   I Have Dreamed
86   We Kiss in a Shadow

THE LIGHT IN THE PIAZZA
90   The Light in the Piazza

MAN OF LA MANCHA
98   What Does He Want of Me

MONTY PYTHON'S SPAMALOT
101   The Song that Goes Like This

MUSIC IN THE AIR
106   The Song Is You

MYTHS AND HYMNS
109   Migratory V

THE NEW MOON
114   Lover, Come Back to Me

110 IN THE SHADE
117   Love, Don't Turn Away

ONE TOUCH OF VENUS
122   Speak Low

PAL JOEY
132   Bewitched

PHANTOM
136   Home

PINS AND NEEDLES
127   Nobody Makes a Pass at Me

PLAIN AND FANCY
142   I'll Show Him

RAGS
150   Children of the Wind

RAGTIME
156   Your Daddy's Son

ROBERTA
170   Yesterdays

1776
161   He Plays the Violin

SHE LOVES ME
172   Vanilla Ice Cream

SHOW BOAT
179   Make Believe
184   Why Do I Love You?

SIMPLE SIMON
191   He Was Too Good to Me

ST. LOUIS WOMAN
194   I Wonder What Became of Me

SWEET ADELINE
212   Why Was I Born?

URINETOWN
198   Follow Your Heart

WONDERFUL TOWN
206   A Little Bit in Love

ABOUT THE SHOWS

*The material in this section is by Stanley Green, Richard Walters, Brian Dean,
and Robert Viagas, some of which was previously published elsewhere.*

BEAUTY AND THE BEAST

MUSIC: Alan Menken
LYRICS: Howard Ashman and Tim Rice
BOOK: Linda Woolverton
DIRECTOR: Robert Jess Roth
CHOREOGRAPHER: Matt West
OPENED: 4/18/94, New York; still running as of December 2005

Disney made its Broadway debut with a big-budget adaptation of its own 1991 Oscar-nominated animated film musical. Like the classic fairy tale on which it is based, *Beauty and the Beast* tells the story of a witch who transforms a haughty prince into a fearsome Beast (and his retainers into household objects). Her spell can be broken only when the prince learns how to love, and how to inspire love. Lyricist Ashman died in 1991 before the film opened. The stage score includes several trunk songs written for the film, but not used, plus five new songs with lyrics by Broadway veteran Rice. Belle is a dreamy, bookish ingenue, a bit of a social outcast in her own way. Much to her surprise she falls in love with the initially brutish Beast. Belle sings "Home," added for the Broadway score, after first being imprisoned in the Beast's castle.

THE BOY FRIEND

MUSIC, LYRICS AND BOOK: Sandy Wilson
DIRECTOR: Cy Feuer
CHOREOGRAPHER: John Heawood
OPENED: 1/14/54, London; a run of 2,084 performances
9/30/54, New York; a run of 485 performances

The Boy Friend is nostalgically set in the roaring twenties, following a mild trend in the 1950s for interest in that era. It evokes the stylized lyrics, melodies and rhythms of the 1920s in its score. Rich lords and ladies summer on the French Riviera. Polly Browne is an heiress who is posing as a commoner, looking for a boy friend not interested in her money. *Sans* companionship at the outset, Polly meets the handsome messenger boy Tony, cutely expressing her feelings for him in the bouncy "I Could Be Happy with You." After a series of misunderstandings and misrepresentations, she eventually learns that Tony is, in fact, an English lord. On the beach at a dance, the peppy French maid Hortense extols the wonders of their glamorous locale in "It's Nicer in Nice." *The Boy Friend* ran to great success in London, and its New York premiere was the Broadway debut for eighteen-year-old Julie Andrews. The 1972 film was adapted rather freely by director Ken Russell, but kept most of the songs intact. It starred fashion model Twiggy and the equally leggy Tommy Tune. *The Boy Friend* has a little performed sequel, written in 1964, called *Divorce Me, Darling.*

BYE BYE BIRDIE

MUSIC: Charles Strouse
LYRICS: Lee Adams
BOOK: Michael Stewart
DIRECTOR AND CHOREOGRAPHER: Gower Champion
OPENED: 4/14/60, New York; a run of 607 performances

The first musical to deal with rock and roll and its effect on the youth, *Bye Bye Birdie* was also the first musical by collaborators Charles Strouse and Lee Adams. Conrad Birdie is the Elvis-inspired pop star who is being drafted. As a publicity stunt before he leaves for the army, his agent decides that he will kiss a young lady live on the Ed Sullivan television show while performing his new song "One Last Kiss." The ingenue of his affection is teenager Kim McAffee. Tempers flare when her current romance is tread upon. During the live broadcast, Birdie is punched out by Kim's jealous boyfriend, before the singer can plant the kiss on Kim. A chase ensues the next day as Birdie tries to get out of town. Early in the show, Kim, recently having stepped down from the presidency of the Conrad Birdie fan club, sings of her burgeoning adulthood in "How Lovely to Be a Woman." After jumping back on the Birdie bandwagon, Kim has to assuage her boyfriend Hugo that she only has eyes for him ("One Boy"). The original production starred Dick Van Dyke, Chita Rivera, Kay Medford and Charles Nelson Reilly. The 1963 movie starred Van Dyke, Janet Leigh, Maureen Stapleton, Paul Lynde, and Ann-Margret. A TV version was made in 1995 with Jason Alexander, Vanessa Williams, and Chynna Phillips. A sequel, *Bring Back Birdie,* by the same authors, had a short run in 1981.

CINDERELLA

MUSIC: Richard Rodgers
LYRICS AND BOOK: Oscar Hammerstein II
DIRECTOR: Ralph Nelson
CHOREOGRAPHER: Jonathan Lucas
FIRST AIRED: 3/31/57 on CBS-TV

Ever the innovators, Rodgers and Hammerstein were among the first to explore the new medium of television with a full-length original TV musical. The show also was fortunate in securing the services of Julie Andrews, fresh from her triumph as the Cinderella-like heroine of *My Fair Lady*. In adapting the children's fairy tale, Hammerstein was careful not to alter or update the familiar story about a young woman whose Fairy Godmother helps her to overcome the plots of her evil stepmother and stepsisters so that she can go to an opulent ball and meet the handsome prince. Cinderella still loses her magical glass slipper, and the Prince still proclaims that he will marry the girl whose foot fits the slipper. "A Lovely Night" is the morning after song of recalling the Prince's ball. Cinderella's stepmother and stepsisters do not understand how she can describe it so perfectly, but they joyfully join in the number. The 1957 live broadcast drew the largest American television audience to date. A 1965 TV production was made in color, starring Lesley Ann Warren. A new production was filmed for ABC-TV starring Brandy, Whitney Houston, Bernadette Peters and others, first airing in 1997. In 2004, a black-and-white kinescope taping of the rehearsal for the original 1957 production starring Julie Andrews was discovered and subsequently released on DVD. A stage adaptation toured the U.S.; the musical finally made its New York stage debut in 1993 at New York City Opera.

A DATE WITH JUDY (film)

MUSIC AND LYRICS: various writers
SCREENPLAY: Dorothy Cooper, Dorothy Kingsley and Aleen Leslie
DIRECTOR: Richard Thorpe
CHOREOGRAPHER: Stanley Donnan
RELEASED: 1948, MGM

Based on the popular, homespun radio program of the same name, which ran from 1941-1950, the MGM movie treatment of *A Date with Judy* starred ingenue Jane Powell in the title role. Judy is a boy crazy teenager, happy to gossip and cajole dates from her hours spent on the telephone. In this droll musical, she has a boyfriend, Oogie, but she changes affections when a new boy, Stephen (Robert Stack), comes to town. Stephen is more interested in the young Carol Pringle (Elizabeth Taylor) who is Oogie's sister. After many colorful mishaps and misunderstandings, including Carmen Miranda teaching Judy's dad (Wallace Beery) to conga, all the characters end up happy in the end. "It's a Most Unusual Day," written by Harold Adamson and Jimmy McHugh, comes back more than once in the movie as a kind of a good-natured audience sing-a-long, first crooned by Powell. A short-lived TV show aired with the same title in 1952.

A DAY IN HOLLYWOOD/A NIGHT IN THE UKRAINE

MUSIC: Frank Lazarus, featuring songs of many others
LYRICS AND BOOK: Dick Vosburgh
DIRECTOR AND CHOREOGRAPHER: Tommy Tune
OPENED: 5/1/80, New York; a run of 588 performances

The slash in the title shows the dual nature of this good-natured revue/musical. The first act is a musical revue, put on by the cinephile ushers at the famous Grauman's Chinese Theater in Hollywood, and includes many well-loved songs such as "Thanks for the Memory." The second act is a movie that is being shown at Grauman's, a madcap, original Marx brothers musical, set in the Ukraine the night before the Revolution (based on Anton Chekhov's 19th century farcical play *The Bear*). In the first act, a Jerry Herman song, "Nelson," lambasts the Nelson Eddy/Jeanette MacDonald movie musical romance, notably in the Canadian Mountie/Opera Singer matchup in 1936's *Rose-Marie* (also known as *Indian Love Call*). An usher, posing as Jeanette, sings about their (Canadian) rocky romance to a life-size cardboard cutout of Nelson.

DRAT! THE CAT!

MUSIC: Milton Schafer
LYRICS AND BOOK: Ira Levin
DIRECTOR AND CHOREOGRAPHER: Joe Layton
OPENED: 10/10/65, New York; a run of 8 performances

Drat! The Cat! is set in 1890s New York City. A cat burglar is on the prowl, thieving from the richest of New York's upper class. Bob Purefoy (Elliot Gould) is the policeman on the case. His first act of prevention is to protect the upper crust party thrown by the Van Guilders. He falls immediately in love with their daughter Alice (Leslie Ann Warren). Little does he know that she is actually the cat burglar he is trying to catch! Her crime spree stems from her rebellion against her parents' wishes for her to settle down and be married. She wants instead to make a career for herself. Slyly, she feigns interest for Purefoy, and even offers to help the policeman to catch the cat. In the end, Purefoy allows her to escape, and she realizes that she actually does have real feelings for him ("I Like Him"). The show had a short run, but gained some notoriety when Barbra Streisand, Gould's wife at the time, recorded a single of his song in the show "She Touched Me" as "He Touched Me." A new studio recording was produced in 1997.

FANNY

MUSIC AND LYRICS: Harold Rome
BOOK: S.N. Berman and Joshua Logan
DIRECTOR: Joshua Logan
CHOREOGRAPHER: Helen Tamiris
OPENED: 11/4/54, New York; a run of 888 performances

Fanny takes us to the colorful, bustling port of Marseilles "not so long ago" for a musical version of Marcel Pagnol's French film trilogy, *Marius, Fanny* and *César* (originally played onscreen by Ezio Pinza). Compressed into an evening's entertainment, the action-packed story concerns Marius, who yearns to go to sea; his father, César, the local café owner; Panisse, a prosperous middle-aged sail maker; and Fanny, the girl beloved by both Marius and Panisse. Though Fanny has a child with Marius just before he ships off, Panisse marries her and brings up the boy as his own. When Marius returns demanding both Fanny and his son, César convinces him that Panisse has the more rightful claim. Years later, however, the dying Panisse dictates a letter to Marius offering him Fanny's hand in marriage. Earlier, seeing that Marius's attention is kept by another girl, Fanny passionately professes her love for Marius in "I Have to Tell You." All of the songs were eliminated for the 1961 screen version directed by Logan.

FLORA, THE RED MENACE

MUSIC: John Kander
LYRICS: Fred Ebb
BOOK: George Abbott and Robert Russell; based on the novel *Love Is Just Around the Corner* by Lester Atwell
DIRECTOR: George Abbott
CHOREOGRAPHER: Lee Theodore
OPENED: 5/11/65, New York; a run of 87 performances

Kander and Ebb had written a handful of successful songs in the early sixties, but *Flora the Red Menace* was their first Broadway musical. It was also the Broadway debut of nineteen-year-old Liza Minelli, starting a lifelong relationship between Liza and the songwriting duo. The show was set in Depression-era New York. Flora (Minelli) is an earnest high school graduate, looking for a job and a way to change the world. She finds work in the art department of Garrett and Melick's, a leading department store. At the same time, she meets and starts to fall for the stammering but incendiary Harry, who is a card carrying Communist. He pressures her to join the party. The show is about Flora balancing the pro-union agenda of her boyfriend's party and her need for a job. A lovely ballad, sung by Liza Minelli when her range was higher and lighter, is a wonderful evocation of first love, not announced brassy and loud as Flora expected, but rather as "A Quiet Thing."

A FUNNY THING HAPPENED ON THE WAY TO THE FORUM

MUSIC AND LYRICS: Stephen Sondheim
BOOK: Burt Shevelove and Larry Gelbart
DIRECTOR: George Abbott
CHOREOGRPAHER: Jack Cole
OPENED: 5/8/62, New York; a run of 964 performances

Full of sight gags, pratfalls, mistaken identity, leggy girls, and other familiar vaudeville ingredients, *Forum* is a bawdy, farcical, pell-mell musical whose likes have seldom been seen on Broadway. Originally intended as a vehicle first for Phil Silvers and then for Milton Berle, *A Funny Thing Happened on the Way to the Forum* opened on Broadway with Zero Mostel as Pseudolus the slave, who is forced to go through a series of mad-cap adventures before being allowed his freedom. Though the show was a hit, things had not looked very promising during the pre-Broadway tryout, and director Jerome Robbins was called in. The most important change: beginning the musical with the song "Comedy Tonight," which set the right mood for the wacky doings that followed. To come up with a script, the librettists researched all twenty-one surviving comedies by the Roman playwright Plautus (254-184 BC), then wrote an original book incorporating such typical characters as the conniving servants, the lascivious master, the domineering mistress, the officious warrior, the simple-minded hero (called Hero), and the senile old man. Both Mostel (as Pseudolus) and Silvers (as Marcus Lycus) were in the 1966 United Artists screen version, along with Jack Gilford and Buster Keaton. The 1997 Broadway revival starred Nathan Lane as Pseudolus; the role was later played by Whoopi Goldberg. Philia is the ingenue slave girl, the object of Hero's affection. Philia's strong suit is that she is absolutely "Lovely," as she tells us in this song.

INTO THE WOODS

MUSIC AND LYRICS: Stephen Sondheim
BOOK AND DIRECTION: James Lapine
CHOREOGRAPHER: Lar Lubovitch
OPENED: 11/5/87, New York; a run of 765 performances

Into the Woods brought together for the second time the Pulitzer Prize winning team of Lapine and Sondheim. Instead of the "art of making art," this time they turned to children's fairy tales as their subject. The book of *Into the Woods* often focuses on the darker, grotesque aspects of these stories, but by highlighting them, it touches on the themes of interpersonal relationships, death, and what we pass on to our children. Act One begins with the familiar "once upon a time" stories, and masterfully interweaves the plots of Snow White, Little Red Riding Hood, Cinderella, Jack and the Beanstalk, a Baker and his Wife and others. Act Two concerns what happens *after* "happily ever after," as reality sets in, and the fairy tale plots dissolve into more human stories. Cinderella evaded the prince earlier in the show. She sings of their second meeting, where she narrowly avoided capture by the prince "On the Steps of the Palace." At the end of the show, the Baker quietly tells his infant son the story of the boy's birth, and the morals we have all learned through the night of theatre. The Witch sings "Children Will Listen" (later joined by the whole ensemble). Though the role of the Witch is principally for a belter, "Children Will Listen" is in a more soprano range, thus suited to this volume. A revival came to Broadway in 2002, starring Vanessa Williams as the Witch.

THE KING AND I

MUSIC: Richard Rodgers
LYRICS AND BOOK: Oscar Hammerstein II
DIRECTOR: John Van Druten
CHOREOGRAPHER: Jerome Robbins
OPENED: 3/29/51, New York; a run of 1,246 performances

The idea of turning Margaret Landon's novel *Anna and the King of Siam* into a musical first occurred to Gertrude Lawrence, who saw it as a suitable vehicle for her return to the Broadway stage. Based on the diaries of an adventurous Englishwoman, the story is set in Bangkok in the early 1860s. Anna Leonowens, who has accepted the post of schoolteacher to the Siamese king's children, has frequent clashes with the monarch, but eventually comes to exert great influence on him, particularly in creating a more democratic society for his people. The show marked the fifth collaboration between Richard Rodgers and Oscar Hammerstein II, their third to run over one thousand performances. Cast opposite Miss Lawrence (who died in 1952 during the run of the play) was the then little-known Yul Brynner. After the original production Brynner virtually made the King his personal property. In 1956, he co-starred with Deborah Kerr in the Fox movie version. Twenty-seven years later, Brynner began touring in a new stage production which played New York in 1977 and London in 1979, eventually performing the role 4,625 times. A new Broadway production opened in 1996, starring Donna Murphy and Lou Diamond Phillips. Tuptim is a beautiful young woman who was given as a gift to the King of Siam by the King of Burma. She is in love with Lun Tha, the Burmese messenger who brought her to Siam. The two of them secretly meet and sing two duets expressing their longing: "We Kiss in a Shadow" and "I Have Dreamed." Both have been adapted as solos for this edition.

THE LIGHT IN THE PIAZZA

MUSIC AND LYRICS: Adam Guettel
BOOK: Craig Lucas, based on the novella of the same name by Elizabeth Spencer
DIRECTOR: Bartlett Sher
CHOREOGRAPHER: Jonathan Butterell
OPENED: 4/18/05, New York; still running as of December 2005

Finding inspiration in the same country as his grandfather Richard Rodgers' *Do I Hear a Waltz?*, Adam Guettel's *The Light in the Piazza* follows Americans abroad in Italy. The plot concerns a mother and her daughter Clara on extended holiday in Florence in 1953. Clara is mentally challenged, having the mind of ten-year-old, but the passions of a young woman. She sings of her pleasure in simple things in "The Light in the Piazza." An Italian man, Fabrizio, falls for the beautiful girl, and much of the story revolves around Clara's mother trying to protect her child from a perceived incompatibility with the young suitor. In the end, Clara and Fabrizio will be married. A non-musical movie treatment was made in 1962, starring Olivia de Havilland and Rossano Brazzi.

MAN OF LA MANCHA

MUSIC: Mitch Leigh
LYRICS: Joe Darion
BOOK: Dale Wasserman
DIRECTOR: Albert Marre
CHOREOGRAPHER: Jack Cole
OPENED: 11/22/65, New York; a run of 2,328 performances

Cervantes' great demented hero, Don Quixote, is the unlikely hero of this popular musical of the 1960s. Although very much rooted in the Spanish novelist's work, this musical version was adapted from Dale Wasserman's television play, *I, Don Quixote*. The principal characters, besides Don Quixote, are Sancho Panza, the Don's squire and sidekick, and Aldonza, who Quixote sees as his grand lady, Dulcinea. Quixote hounds the fierce Aldonza with his overtures of love; she in turn continually spurns him. As her heart gradually thaws, she wonders, "What Does He Want of Me?" The film version, released in 1972, starred Peter O'Toole and Sophia Loren. *Man of La Mancha* has returned several times to Broadway, with revivals in 1972, 1977, 1992, and 2002.

MONTY PYTHON'S SPAMALOT

MUSIC: John Du Prez and Eric Idle
LYRICS: Eric Idle
BOOK: Eric Idle, "lovingly ripped off from the motion picture *Monty Python and the Holy Grail*"
DIRECTOR: Mike Nichols
CHOREOGRAPHER: Casey Nicholaw
OPENED: 3/17/05, New York; still running as of December 2005

Eric Idle, one of the founding members of the British television comedy troupe "Monty Python's Flying Circus," made his Broadway writing debut with *Monty Python's Spamalot*, billed as "a new musical lovingly ripped off from the motion picture *Monty Python and the Holy Grail*." As in the movie, the show involves the wacky adventures of King Arthur and his band of knights in their search for the Holy Grail, shrubbery, and in the musical, success on the Great White Way. The lavish *Spamalot* was directed by luminary Broadway and movie director Mike Nichols. The original cast starred Tim Curry, Hank Azaria, and David Hyde Pierce. True to characteristic Python irreverence and silliness, *Spamalot* lambasts the musical genre at every step, one such example being the aptly named "The Song that Goes Like This," sung by The Lady of the Lake and Sir Dennis Galahad. The song has been adapted as a solo for this edition.

MUSIC IN THE AIR

MUSIC: Jerome Kern
LYRICS AND BOOK: Oscar Hammerstiein II
DIRECTOR: Jerome Kern and Oscar Hammerstein II
OPENED: 11/8/32, New York, a run of 342 performances

A "show within a show," *Music in the Air* reunited *Show Boat* writers Jerome Kern and Oscar Hammerstein. In the small Bavarian town of Edendorf, a music teacher, Walther, begins a trek to Munich to try to get his songs published. He is joined by his daughter, Sieglinde, and her soon-to-be sweetheart Karl. Once in Munich they become mixed up in the middle of an operetta production, and a rocky relationship between the diva Frieda, and her lover, the librettist/impresario Bruno. Outraged by the attention Bruno gives young Sieglinde, Frieda storms out of the production, and attempts to take the handsome Karl with her. Undaunted by the chaos surrounding his operetta, librettist Bruno continually tries to win the heart of Sieglinde, as in the duet "The Song Is You" (here presented as a soprano solo). The young country girl ends up being cast in the lead role, but against expectations in musical theatre, she doesn't have the skills to save the show! Father, daughter and Karl end up back in Edendorf to a happy ending of published songs and young love. A movie was made in 1934, with Gloria Swanson in the diva's role.

MYTHS AND HYMNS

MUSIC, LYRICS AND BOOK: Adam Guettel
DIRECTOR: Tina Landau
OPENED: 3/31/98, New York; a run of 16 performances

The source material for Guettel's *Myths and Hymns* is just that—mythological figures such as Icarus, Pegasus and Sisyphus, and old texts from an 1886 Presbyterian Hymnal Guettel found in a used book store. The song cycle for the theatre premiered under the name *Saturns Returns* but was later changed to the present title. *Floyd Collins* director Landau helped stage this night of music, which focused on the divine and profane in everyday life and uses musical language from straight-up pop to lush theatrical writing. "Migratory V" acknowledges our solitary achievements, but asks if we can come together in one voice, as does a flock of birds, can we not achieve a glimpse of the eternal?

THE NEW MOON

MUSIC: Sigmund Romberg
LYRICS: Oscar Hammerstein II
BOOK: Oscar Hammerstein II, Frank Mandel and Laurence Schwab
DIRECTOR: Edgar MacGregor (uncredited)
CHOREOGRAPHER: Bobby Connolly
OPENED: 9/19/28, New York; a run of 509 performances

Hammerstein and Romberg's follow up to their popular *Desert Song* had everything from young love and marriage to murder, double crossing, piracy, and revolution. *The New Moon* is a sprawling musical, set in French Colonial New Orleans, on the ship the New Moon, and on the Isle of Pines. Noble born Robert Mission killed the King of France's cousin, and had himself sold into bondage as cover to escape to America. The plot follows Robert's attempt to gain stouthearted supporters against the King, and to woo the hand of the beautiful Marianne, the daughter of the household where he is indentured. Vicomte Ribaud is sent from France to track down the lawless Mission. Robert is caught and is being extradited to France on the New Moon, along with Marianne, who has come along because she has been engaged for years to the ship's inept captain Georges. While onboard, she writes Robert a love note reading, "Lover, Come Back to Me." Sympathizers of Robert, in the guise of pirates, attack the ship and rescue him, and he leads them to the Isle of Pines, where they will try to live Robert's utopian, nationalistic vision. Ribaud is still with them, and he secretly summons two French ships to the island to rescue himself and catch Robert for the second time. When the ships arrive, they bring news that more revolution has occurred in France, and Robert's loyalty to the country but defiance of the King is saluted. Robert will stay to rule the Isle of Pines with Marianne by his side. A movie starring Jeanette MacDonald and Nelson Eddy was released in 1940.

110 IN THE SHADE

MUSIC: Harvey Schmidt
LYRCS: Tom Jones
BOOK: N. Richard Nash
DIRECTOR: Joseph Anthony
CHOREOGRAPHER: Agnes De Mille
OPENED: 10/24/63, New York; a run of 330 performances

N. Richard Nash adapted his play, *The Rainmaker*, for Schmidt and Jones' first Broadway musical, following their wildly successful Off-Broadway musical *The Fantasticks*. Nash's play is probably best remembered for the film version which starred Burt Lancaster and Katharine Hepburn. It is a simple tale of Lizzie, an aging, unmarried woman who lives with her father and brothers on a drought-stricken ranch in the American west. Starbuck, a transient "rainmaker," comes on the scene and is soon viewed to be the con man that he is, despite his dazzling charisma. He does, however, pay somewhat sincere attention to Lizzie, and awakens love and life in her. Nevertheless, she sees no future with Starbuck, and winds up with a reliable local suitor instead. The show was featured in a prominent production by New York City Opera in 1992. Lizzies's first song, "Love Don't Turn Away," implores love to not pass by her "open arms that are aching for their first embrace."

ONE TOUCH OF VENUS

MUSIC: Kurt Weill
LYRICS: Ogden Nash
BOOK: S.J. Perelman and Ogden Nash
DIRECTOR: Elia Kazan
CHOREOGRAPHER: Agnes De Mille
OPENED: 10/7/43, New York; a run of 567 performances

One Touch of Venus gathered together many of Broadway's best—the prolific Kurt Weill, witty Ogden Nash in his first and only book musical, celebrated motion picture and Broadway director Elia Kazan, choreographer Agnes De Mille, and Mary Martin in her second musical and first starring role, as the statue come to life. At one time, Marlene Dietrich was considered for the role of Venus. A rich patron in the arts, Whitelaw Savory, imports a statue of Venus to his foundation. His barber, Rodney Hatch, absent-mindedly places the engagement ring meant for his fiancée Gloria upon the ring of Venus, which brings her to life, and makes her fall in love with him. Venus experiences present day New York while pursuing Rodney, and being chased by the old man Savory. In her quest to entice Rodney, she also banishes the meddlesome Gloria to the North Pole. Though at first staying true to the acerbic Gloria, Rodney eventually succumbs to the wiles of Venus, as she beckons him to come to her and "Speak Low." The production was marked by beautiful, New York inspired ballets by De Mille, such as "Forty Minutes for Lunch." A movie version was released in 1948 starring Ava Gardner.

PAL JOEY

MUSIC: Richard Rodgers
LYRICS: Lorenz Hart
BOOK: John O'Hara
DIRECTOR: George Abbott
CHOREOGRAPHER: Robert Alton
OPENED: 12/25/40; a run of 374 performances

With its heel for a hero, its smoky night-club atmosphere, and its true-to-life characters, *Pal Joey* was a major breakthrough in bringing about a more adult form of musical theatre. Adapted by John O'Hara from his own *New Yorker* short stories, the show is about Joey Evans, an entertainer at a small Chicago nightclub, who is attracted to the innocent Linda English, but drops her in favor of a wealthy, middle-aged Vera Simpson. Vera builds a glittering nightclub, the Chez Joey, for her paramour but she soon grows tired of him, and Joey, at the end, is on his way to other conquests. In his only major Broadway role, Gene Kelly got the chance to sing "I Could Write a Book," and Vivienne Segal, as Vera, introduced "Bewitched." Vera is wise to Joey, but enjoys their affair. The comic-naughty song "Bewitched" was given a different, sanitized lyric by Hart for its life apart from the show and became a popular standard. Though it had a respectable run, *Pal Joey* was considered somewhat ahead of its time when it was first produced. A 1952 Broadway revival, with Miss Segal repeating her original role and Harold Lang as Joey, received a more appreciative reception and went on to a run of 542 performances. In 1957, Columbia made a film version (a loose adaptation), with George Sidney directing, starring Frank Sinatra, Kim Novak and Rita Hayworth.

PHANTOM

MUSIC AND LYRICS: Maury Yeston
BOOK: Arthur Kopit, from the novel *The Phantom of the Opera* by Gaston Leroux
OPENED: 1991, Houston

Yeston's *Phantom* has never had a Broadway run, but it has played widely in the United States, receiving raves from critics in Chicago, Boston, New York, Houston and other places. Yeston and Kopit actually wrote their show before Lloyd Webber wrote his, but were unable to get any financing for a Broadway production after the British musical was announced. Yeston, composer of *Nine, Grand Hotel,* and *Titanic,* was once a music textbook author and professor at Yale, and also composed a cello concerto for Yo-Yo Ma. The story of *Phantom* is familiar. Young ingenue Christine Daae works her way from obscurity to a starring role in the Paris Opera house with help from the menacing and manipulative Phantom. When she first sets foot on stage, only a costume girl at the time, she sings of the thrill she feels as she knows she is "Home."

PINS AND NEEDLES

MUSIC AND LYRICS: Harold Rome
BOOK: Arthur Arent, Marc Blitzstein, Emmanuel Eisenberg, Charles Friedman, David Gregory,
    Joseph Schrank, Arnold B. Horwitt, John Latouche, Harold Rome
DIRECTOR: Charles Friedman
CHOREOGRAPHER: Benjamin Zemach
OPENED: 11/27/37, New York; a run of 1,108

Harold Rome was a prolific songwriter in the 1930s, though his often politically slanted songs were not widely known. Enter the International Ladies Garment Workers Union, and soon Rome would be a star. The ILGWU held meetings in the Princess Theatre, and they decided to put on an inexpensive revue for fun. *Pins and Needles* began to take form when the young Rome was brought in to write his catchy songs. The musical, a mix of story, songs and skits looking at current events through union eyes (and a socialist spirit of the era), was written by, among others, John Latouche and Marc Blitzstein. The show became a runaway hit, and is the only non-union, "union" musical to succeed on Broadway, owing some of its longevity to keeping itself topical by introducing a new skit or song every few months to keep it fresh. A studio recording, produced by Rome in 1962, starred Barbra Streisand, who in the same year would make her Broadway debut in Rome's *I Can Get It For You Wholesale.* "Nobody Makes a Pass at Me" is the lament of a woman who, despite her best efforts at primping and preening, still fails attract a man. Today it is a charming, anachronistic survey of the products used in the 1930s.

PLAIN AND FANCY

MUSIC: Albert Hague
LYRICS: Arnold B. Horwitt
BOOK: Joseph Stein and Will Glickman
DIRECTOR: Morton Da Costa
CHOREOGRPAHER: Helen Tamiris
OPENED: 1/27/55, New York; a run of 461 performances

The setting of *Plain and Fancy* is Amish country in Pennsylvania, where two worldly New Yorkers (Richard Derr and Shirl Conway) have gone to sell a farm they had inherited—but not before they had a chance to meet the local people and appreciate their simple but unyielding way of living. The warm and atmospheric score was composed by Albert Hague, familiar as the bearded music teacher in the film and TV series *Fame.* A young Barbara Cook, in her second Broadway show, plays the part of Amish girl Hilda, who is arranged to be married to a much older man. Furious at her situation, she thumbs her nose at her betrothed and tradition in "I'll Show Him."

RAGS

MUSIC: Charles Strouse
LYRICS: Stephen Schwartz
BOOK: Joseph Stein
DIRECTOR: Gene Saks
CHOREOGRAPHER: Ron Field
OPENED: 8/21/86, New York, a run of 4 performances

On paper, *Rags* looked like a sure hit, with music by Charles Strouse (*Bye Bye Birdie, Annie*), lyrics by Stephen (*Godspell*) Schwartz, a book by *Fiddler on the Roof*'s Joseph Stein, and starring operatic diva Teresa Stratas. However, this sprawling musical, set in 1910 in New York's Lower East Side, and chronicling the lives of the Jewish immigrants who made their way there, could not find favor in its short Broadway run. The score features a wide range of music including Klezmer, Ragtime, and musical comedy. The show has found a new life in many revivals over the years. Rebecca (Stratas) and her young son come to America to reunite with her husband, who has already made the passage from Russia. In "Children of the Wind" she likens the spreading of her family, and all refugees, to being tossed about by the wind.

RAGTIME

MUSIC: Stephen Flaherty
LYRICS: Lynn Ahrens
BOOK: Terrence McNally, from the novel by E.L. Doctorow
DIRECTOR: Frank Galati
CHOREOGRAPHER: Graciela Daniele
OPENED: 1/18/98, New York, a run of 834 performances

Ahrens and Flaherty's *Ragtime* takes its book from the popular novel by E.L. Doctorow about the immigrant experience. A stellar cast, including Audra MacDonald and Brian Stokes Mitchell, helped propel the Broadway run. Set at the turn of the 20th century, this musical has a large cast with many interwoven storylines as the characters move from the time of horse-drawn carriages into the modern age of the automobile. This dense plot pits poor immigrants side by side with Henry Ford, Booker T. Washington, Admiral Perry and J.P. Morgan. Sarah (MacDonald) is a poor African-American mother who has just given birth to a son. His father, the ragtime pianist Coalhouse Walker Jr., left Sarah before he knew she was pregnant. A rich woman finds the child, left in her garden where Sarah tried to abandon him, just as the police arrive with the now mute mother. The woman takes pity on her, and agrees to take care of Sarah and the child. She sings the lullaby of remorse, "Your Daddy's Hands," to her infant son, who, despite Sarah's attempt to forget his father, reminds her of him.

ROBERTA

MUSIC: Jerome Kern
LYRICS AND BOOK: Otto Harbach
DIRECTOR: Hassard Short
CHOREOGRAPHER: José Limon
OPENED: 11/18/33, New York; a run 295 performances

The musical was adapted from Alice Duer Miller's novel *Gowns by Roberta*, but in the end, the little plot that remained in the show seems to be a scant framework for some first rate songs. *Roberta* is probably best remembered as the source for its most famous song, "Smoke Gets in Your Eyes." Vaudeville star Bob Hope had his first major Broadway musical role in the production. "Yesterdays," which had little to do with the story of an American football player who inherits a Paris salon, laments the present melancholy of a lover who had better luck in the past. Two film versions were made of the show: a 1935 version which starred Irene Dunne, Fred Astaire and Ginger Rogers, and *Lovely to Look At* in 1952.

1776

MUSIC AND LYRICS: Sherman Edwards
BOOK: Peter Stone
DIRECTOR: Peter Hunt
CHOREOGRAPHER: Onna White
OPENED: 3/16/69, New York; a run of 1,217 performances

Sherman Edwards' background as a high school history teacher made him a perfect choice to bring the American Revolution to the Broadway stage. Edwards' characters of our heritage leap off the page and their real personalities shine through—the disliked firebrand John Adams, the quiet lover Thomas Jefferson, and the witty Benjamin Franklin, among many others. The cast consists of largely the signers of the Declaration of Independence. We see the fierce debates over states rights, individual autonomy and slavery in the hot Philadelphia days of that defining year. Much of the dialogue is taken verbatim from memoirs and letters of the actual participants. *1776* is not a typical musical with large dance numbers and many songs. It allows ample time for the plot to unfold, and often there are very long breaks with no music as the delegates debate in Congress. Remarkably enough, the florid writer Jefferson is portrayed as a man of few words. When his wife Martha Jefferson is asked how he found the words to propose to her, she replies that it was through music that he won her heart ("He Plays the Violin"). The 1972 movie, directed by Hunt, kept many of the original Broadway actors including, William Daniels (Adams), Ken Howard (Jefferson) and Howard Da Silva (Franklin). A Broadway revival was staged in 1997.

SHE LOVES ME

MUSIC: Jerry Bock
LYRICS: Sheldon Harnick
BOOK: Joe Matsteroff
DIRECTOR: Harold Prince
CHOREOGRPAHER: Carol Haney
OPENED: 4/23/63, New York; a run of 302 performances

The closely integrated, melody drenched score of *She Loves Me* is certainly one of the best ever written for a musical comedy. It was based on a Hungarian play, *Parfumerie*, by Miklos Laszlo, that had already been used as the basis for two films, *The Shop Around the Corner* (1940), and, adapted to an American setting, *In the Good Old Summertime* (1949). Set in the 1930s in what could only be Budapest, the tale is of the people who work in Maraczek's Parfumerie, principally the constantly squabbling sales clerk Amalia Balash (Barbara Cook) and the manager Georg Nowack (Daniel Massey). It is soon revealed that they are anonymous, amorous pen pals who agree to meet one night at the Café Imperiale, though neither knows the other's identity. That evening Georg realizes that it is Amalia who is waiting for him at the restaurant, but he doesn't let on. She is so disheartened that she calls in sick the next day. Georg brings her ice cream and is especially gentle to her, while also planting doubts about her "dear friend" pen pal. Could he be bald, or fat, or old? She ponders Georg's visit in "Vanilla Ice Cream." *She Loves Me*, which would have starred Julie Andrews had she not been filming *Mary Poppins*, was one of Barbara Cook's most magical portrayals. A Broadway revival opened in 1993. The same basic story was adapted for the 1998 film *You've Got Mail*.

SHOW BOAT

MUSIC: Jerome Kern
LYRICS AND BOOK: Oscar Hammerstein II
DIRECTOR: Zeke Colvan and Oscar Hammerstein II
CHOREOGRAPHER: Sammy Lee
OPENED: 12/27/27, New York; a run of 572 performances

No show ever to hit Broadway was more historically important, and at the same time more beloved than *Show Boat*, that landmark of the 1927 season. Edna Ferber's novel of life on the Mississippi was the source for this musical/operetta, and provided a rich plot and characters which Kern and Hammerstein amplified to become some of the most memorable ever to grace the stage. *Show Boat* not only summed up of all that had come before it, both in the musical and operetta genres, and in a distinctly American style, but additionally planted a seed of complete congruity which would later blossom in the more adventurous shows of the '30s, '40s and '50s. Since its premiere in 1927, the show has been in constant revival in some way or another, whether in its three film versions, in New York productions, in touring companies, in operatic repertories, or in the many, many amateur productions. A major Broadway revival opened in 1994. At their first meeting, Ravenal mistakenly thinks Magnolia an actress; she is not (yet), but is happy to "Make Believe" with him. The opening number of the second act, "Why Do I Love You?" has the incredulous newlyweds Ravenal and Magnolia brimming with love for each other.

SIMPLE SIMON

MUSIC: Richard Rodgers
LYRICS: Lorenz Hart
BOOK: Ed Wynn and Guy Bolton
DIRECTOR: Zeke Colvan
CHOREOGRAPHER: Seymour Felix
OPENED: 2/18/30, New York; a run of 135 performances

Simple Simon was a musical comedy meant to showcase the talents of Broadway legend Ed Wynn. In this Ziegfeld production, Wynn plays Simon, a newspaper vendor who enjoys a good fairy tale over a good headline. Most of the show is a dream of Simon's, which takes place in two fantasy kingdoms and involves King Cole, Cinderella, Prince Charming and even the Trojan Horse. Interestingly enough, two of the more famous songs from the production, "Dancing on the Ceiling" and the torch song "He Was Too Good to Me," were cut before the show opened, both probably written for Ruth Etting. This style of musical in this period typically had little character-driven plot context for songs.

ST. LOUIS WOMAN

MUSIC: Harold Arlen
LYRICS: Johnny Mercer
BOOK: Arna Bontemps and Countee Cullen
DIRECTOR: Rouben Mamoulian
CHOREOGRAPHER: Charles Walters
OPENED: 3/30/46, New York; a run of 113 performances

St. Louis Woman, based on Arna Bontemps novel, *God Sends Sunday,* was something of a non-operatic *Porgy and Bess*. Set in 1898, it tells of a fickle St. Louis woman, Della Green, who is first the girlfriend of saloon-keeper Bigelow Brown, then falls for Li'l Augie, a jockey with an incredible winning streak. Before Brown is killed by a rejected lover, he puts a curse on Li'l Augie which ends the winning steak and cools Della's affection. The lovers are, however, reunited for the final singing of their impassioned duet, "Come Rain or Come Shine." In 1959, a revised version of *St. Louis Woman*, relocated to New Orleans and retitled *Free and Easy*, was performed in Amsterdam and Paris. "I Wonder What Became of Me," sung by the melancholy character Leah, is a rarely heard ballad from the composer of "Over the Rainbow."

SWEET ADELINE

MUSIC: Jerome Kern
LYRICS AND BOOK: Oscar Hammerstein II
DIRECTOR: Reginald Hammerstein
CHOREOGRAPHER: Danny Dare
OPENED: 9/3/29, New York; a run of 234 performances

Sweet Adeline paired Jerome Kern and Oscar Hammerstein for the first time since their 1927 smash *Show Boat,* and was intended as a vehicle for Helen Morgan, the original Julie in *Show Boat*. Set in and around New York in 1898, the story concerns Addie Schmidt, the daughter of a Hoboken beer garden owner, and her three loves. After Tom Martin has gone to fight in the Spanish-American war, Addie, now known as Adeline Belmont, becomes a Broadway star and falls for wealthy socialite James Day. But his family disapproves and she happily ends up in the arms of composer Sid Barnett. The show was a family affair for Oscar, produced by his uncle Arthur, and playing in his theatre, and also directed by his brother Reginald. The show capitalized on the brief resurgence of 1890s trends in the 1930s. Down on her luck and blue, a lovesick Adeline melodramatically ponders, "Why Was I Born?" A movie version starring Irene Dunne was released in 1935.

URINETOWN

MUSIC: Mark Hollmann
LYRICS: Mark Hollmann and Greg Kotis
BOOK: Greg Kotis
DIRECTOR: John Rando
CHOREOGRAPHER: John Carrafa
OPENED: 9/20/01, New York; a run of 965 performances

Without seeing the show, it is hard to believe a production called *Urinetown* would come to Broadway, but it did, and had a successful run at that. Greg Kotis had the seed of the idea while broke in Europe and faced with a Parisian pay-per-use toilet. This helped him envision the drought stricken world where a greedy conglomerate, Urine Good Company, owns all the toilets in the city, thus making it a "Privilege to Pee." This show delights in its self-awareness and lambasting of the musical genre, with intentionally cheesy lyrics and a wee plot. Bobby Strong helps the masses to overthrow the corrupt company, while falling for the boss's daughter Hope. She gives him advice, after the jailing of his own father Old Man Strong, to "Follow Your Heart." The show's original opening date of September 13, 2001, was postponed due to the World Trade Center attacks.

WONDERFUL TOWN

MUSIC: Leonard Bernstein
LYRICS: Betty Comden and Adolph Green
BOOK: Joseph A. Fields and Jerome Chodorov
DIRECTOR: George Abbott
CHOREOGRAPHER: Donald Saddler
OPENED: 2/25/53, New York; a run of 559 performances

Wonderful Town reunited the creative team that made 1944's *On the Town* so successful: Bernstein, Comden and Green, and director George Abbott. Set in New York, this show is not a sequel; rather it is based on the hit Broadway play *My Sister Eileen*, which itself was based on Ruth McKinney's semi-autobiographical *New Yorker* short stories. The musical was conceived as a showcase for Rosiland Russell as Ruth. Ruth and Eileen are two sisters making their way in Greenwich Village, originally from a small town in Ohio. Ruth is a writer, and Eileen is…well, pretty. As Ruth chases the story, Eileen is chased by suitor after suitor. Ruth's editor, Bob Baker, comes over to apologize for being curt with Ruth, and Eileen immediately falls "A Little Bit in Love" with him. After a raucous night with seven amorous, Conga-dancing Brazillian naval cadets that lands Eileen in jail, all is well in the end as she realizes that Ruth and Bob love one another, and Eileen finds a singing career. A revival came to Broadway in 2002, with Donna Murphy as Ruth and Jennifer Westfeldt as Eileen.

HOME
from Walt Disney's *Beauty and the Beast: The Broadway Musical*

Music by ALAN MENKEN
Lyrics by TIM RICE

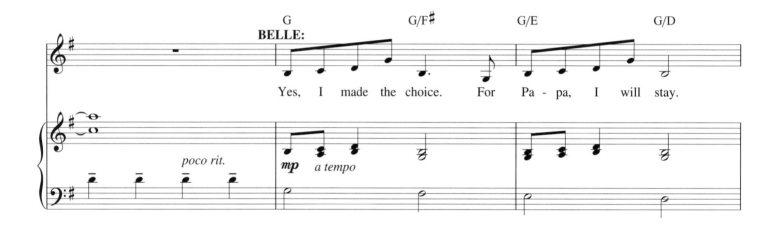

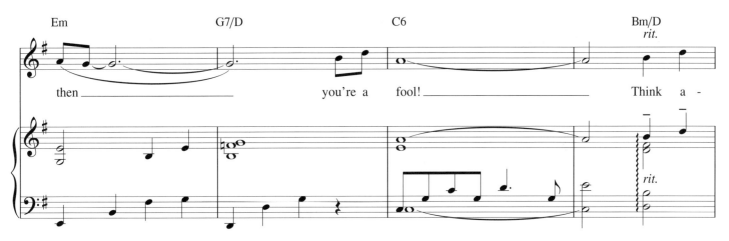

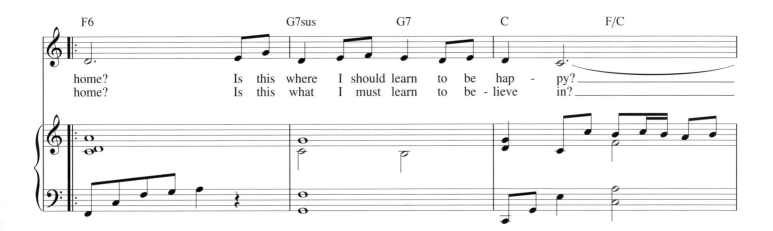

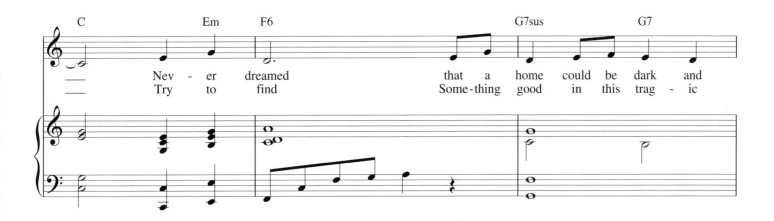

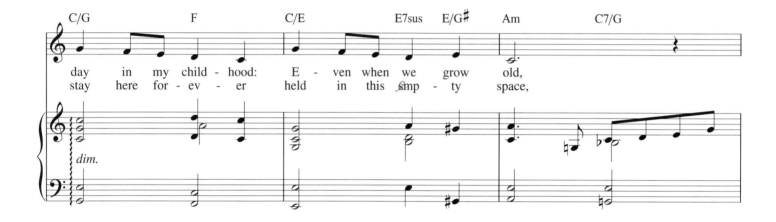

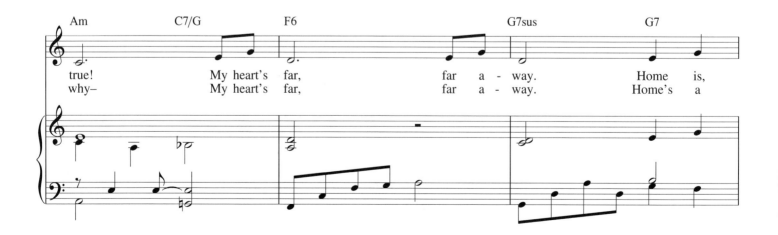

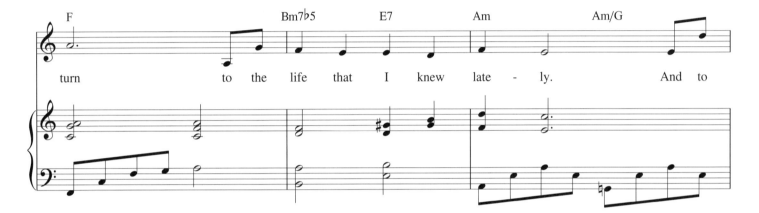

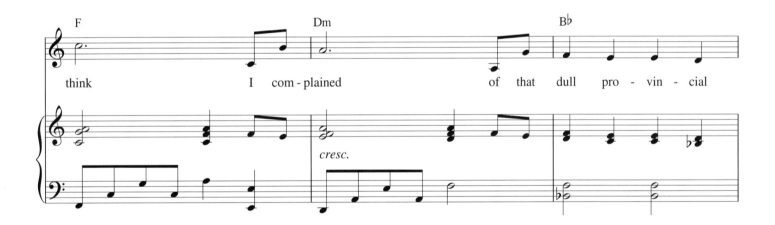

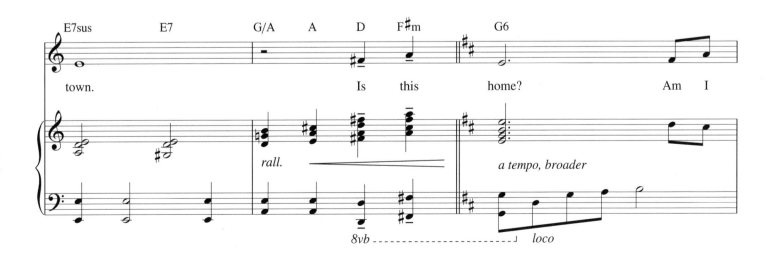

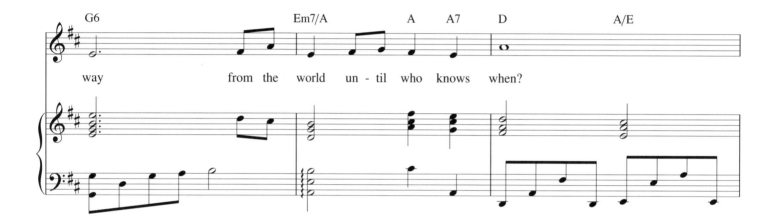

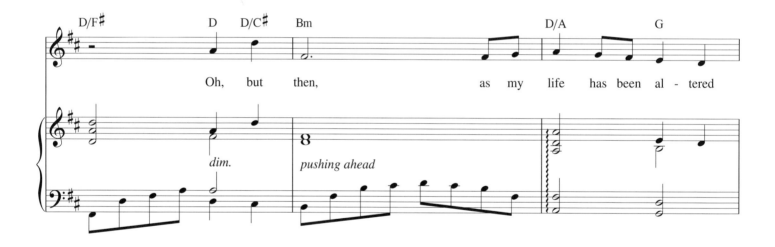

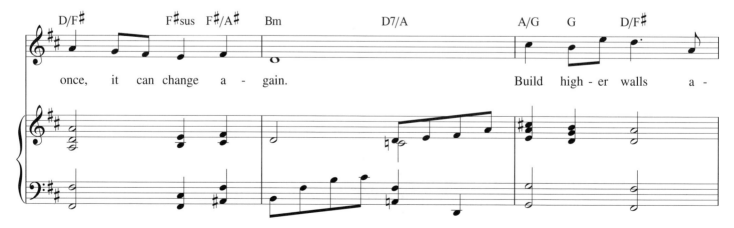

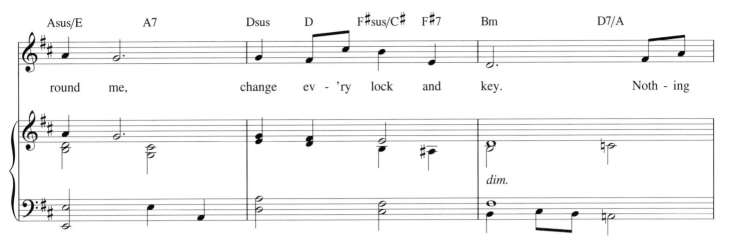

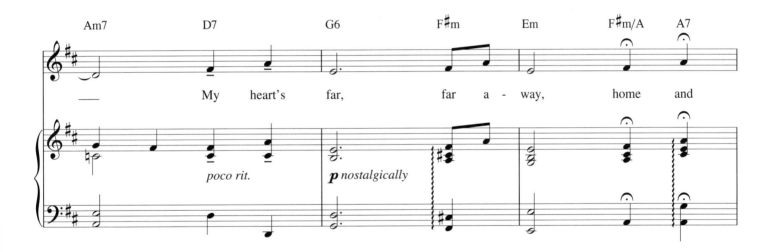

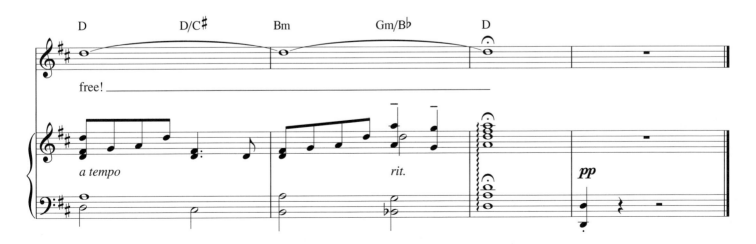

I COULD BE HAPPY WITH YOU

from *The Boy Friend*

Words and Music by
SANDY WILSON

This song is a duet for Polly and Tony in the show, adapted as a solo for this edition.

I'm not one to make pre - dic - tions, but I've thrown off all re - stric-tions And

don't mind con - fess - ing I think it's a bless - ing That you are here.

Though I'm pre - pared to find I'm wrong, _____ I've

legato

rall.

got a fun - ny feel - ing we be - long To - geth - er.

rall.

I could be hap - py with you _____ If

you could be hap - py with me. _____

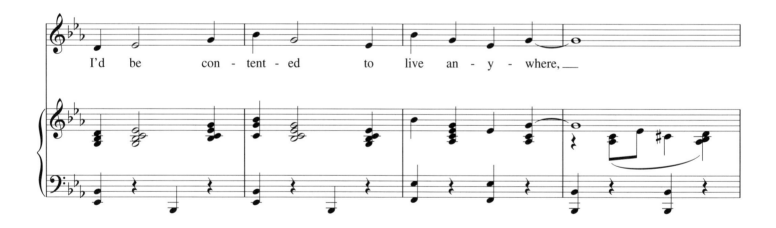

I'd be con - tent - ed to live an - y - where, __

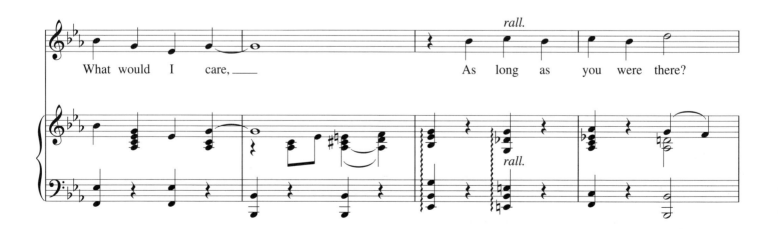

What would I care, __ As long as you were there?

Skies may not al - ways be blue, _____ But

one thing is clear as can be, _____ I know that

I could be hap - py with you, My dar - ling. If

(optional repeat)

you could be hap - py with me.

* *The companion accompaniment CD omits the optional repeat.*

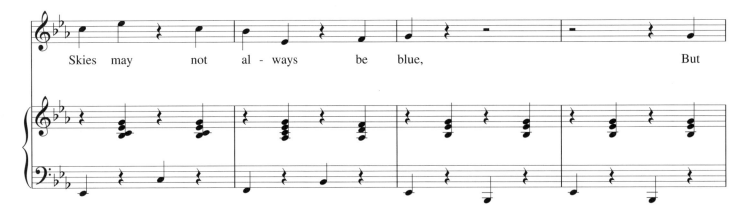

Skies may not al - ways be blue, But

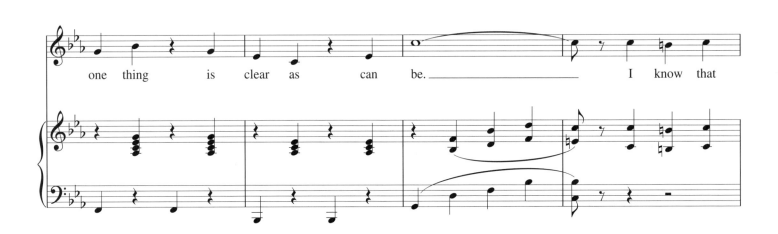

one thing is clear as can be._____ I know that

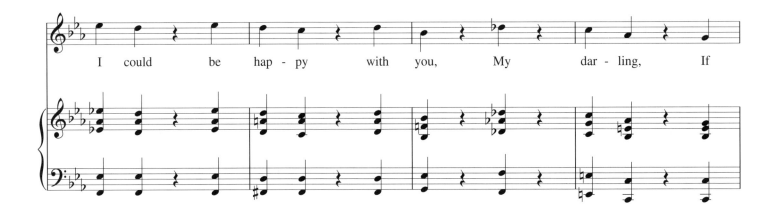

I could be hap - py with you, My dar - ling, If

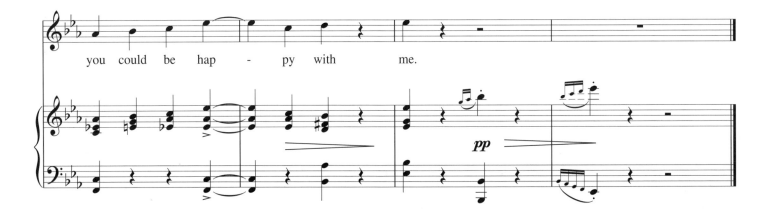

you could be hap - py with me.

IT'S NICER IN NICE
from *The Boy Friend*

Words and Music by
SANDY WILSON

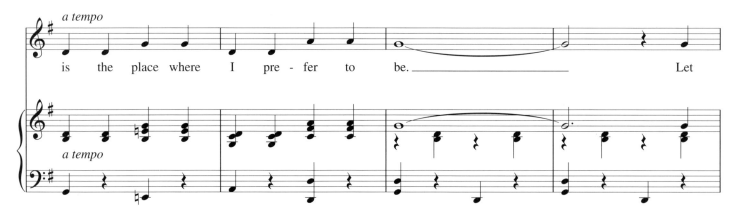

is the place where I pre-fer to be. _____ Let

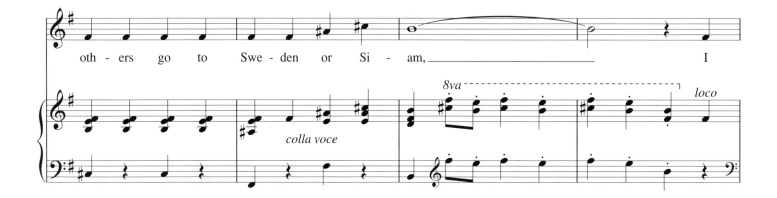

oth-ers go to Swe-den or Si-am, _____ I

think I'll stay ex-act-ly where I am. _____ They

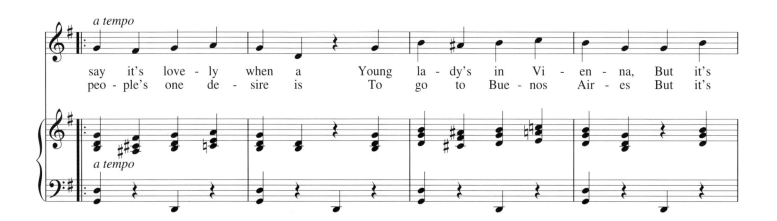

say it's love-ly when a Young la-dy's in Vi-en-na, But it's

peo-ple's one de-sire is To go to Bue-nos Air-es But it's

nic - er, much nic - er in Nice, In
nic - er, much nic - er in Nice, The

Am - ster - dam or Brus - sels The men have great big mus - cles, But they're nic - er, much
laws are rath - er vague in The town of Cop - en - hag - en But they're nic - er, much

nic - er in Nice. I've heard that the I -
nic - er in Nice. And some may like a

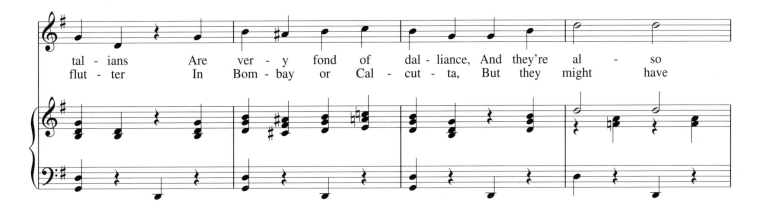

tal - ians Are ver - y fond of dal - liance, And they're al - so
flut - ter In Bom - bay or Cal - cut - ta, But they might have

(2nd time only)

keen on it in Greece.
trou - ble with the p'lice. Oh, la, la! Oth - er plac - es may be

But what - ev - er they may

say, this is where I want to stay, For it's so much nic - er in
fun, but when all is said and done It is so much nic - er in

Nice. Some

Nice. But they

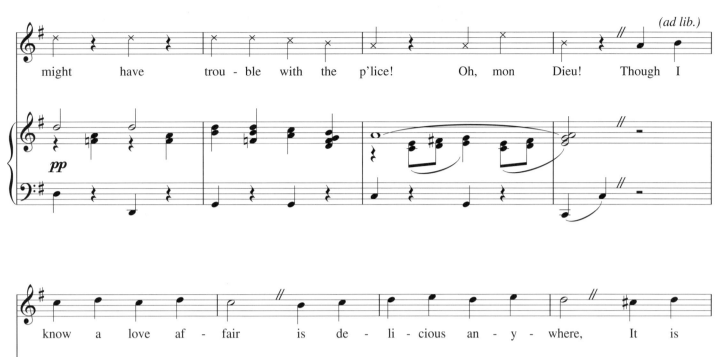

(ad lib.)

might have trou - ble with the p'lice! Oh, mon Dieu! Though I

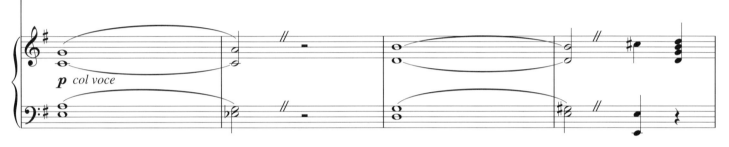

know a love af - fair is de - li - cious an - y - where, It is

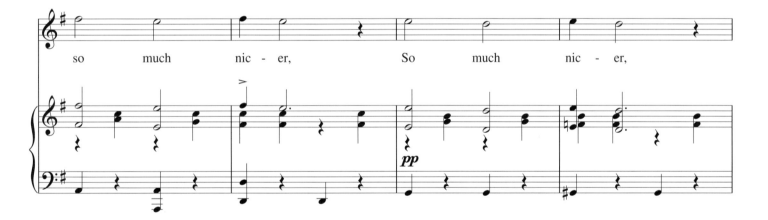

so much nic - er, So much nic - er,

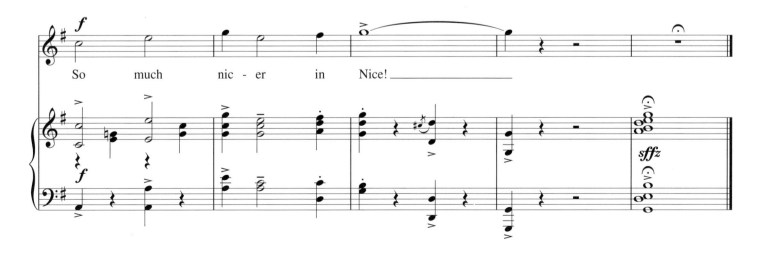

So much nic - er in Nice! _____

HOW LOVELY TO BE A WOMAN
from *Bye Bye Birdie*

Lyric by LEE ADAMS
Music by CHARLES STROUSE

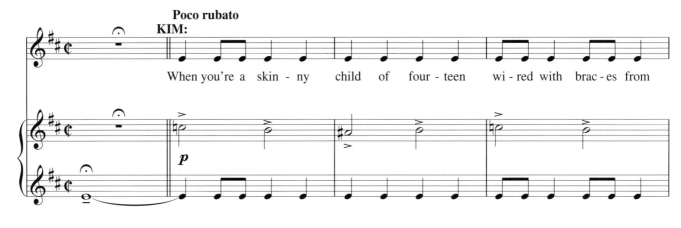

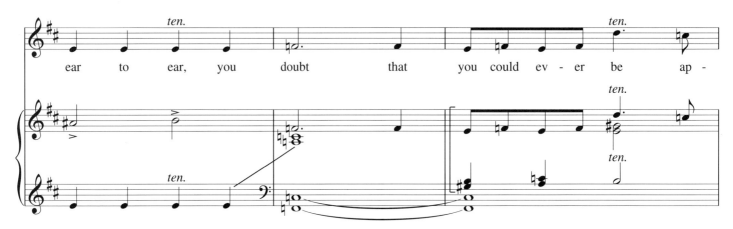

When you're a skin-ny child of four-teen wi-red with brac-es from ear to ear, you doubt that you could ev-er be ap-peal-ing

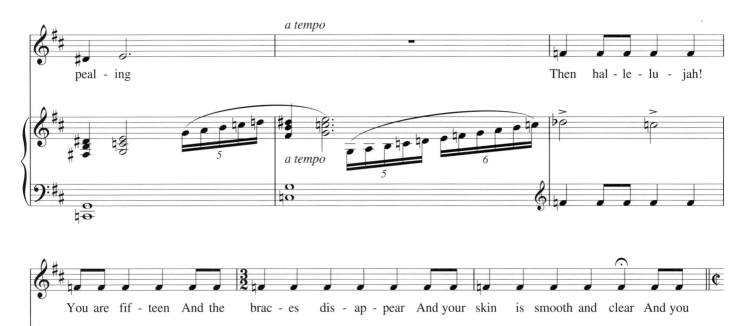

Then hal-le-lu-jah!

You are fif-teen And the brac-es dis-ap-pear And your skin is smooth and clear And you

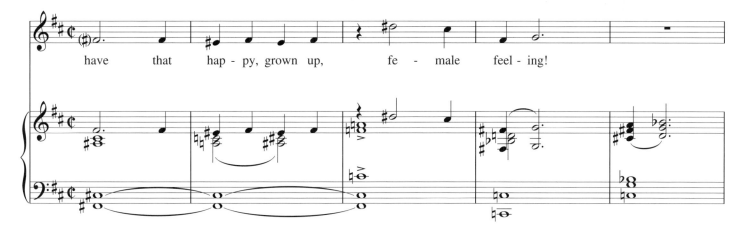

have that hap - py, grown up, fe - male feel - ing!

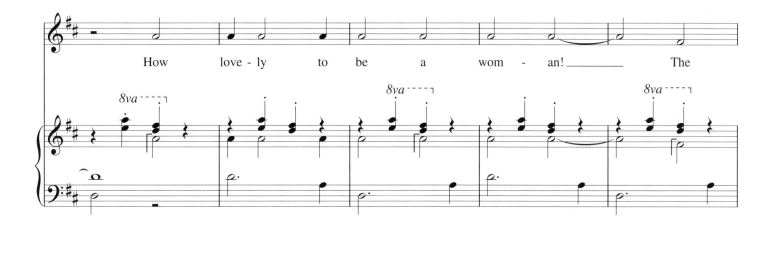

How love - ly to be a wom - an! _____ The

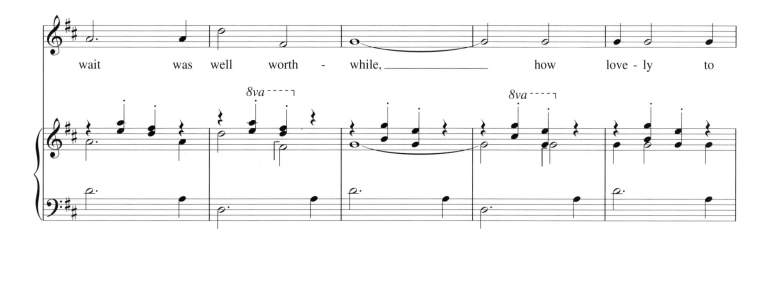

wait was well worth - while, _____ how love - ly to

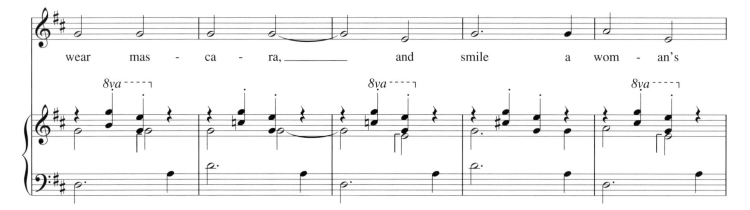

wear mas - ca - ra, _____ and smile a wom - an's

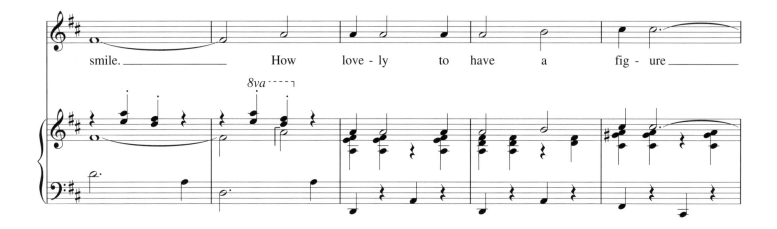

smile. _____ How love - ly to have a fig - ure _____

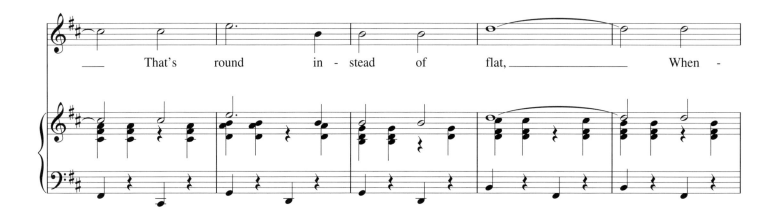

___ That's round in - stead of flat, _____ When -

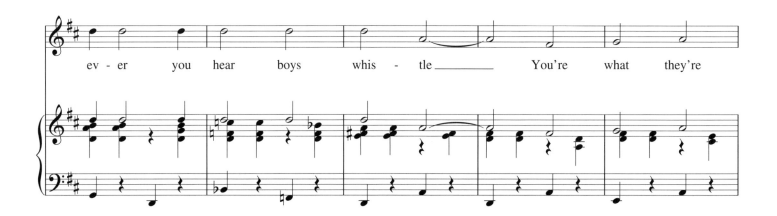

ev - er you hear boys whis - tle _____ You're what they're

whis - tling at! It's won-der-ful to feel _____

_____ The way a wom-an feels, _____ It

gives you such a glow Just to know _____ You're

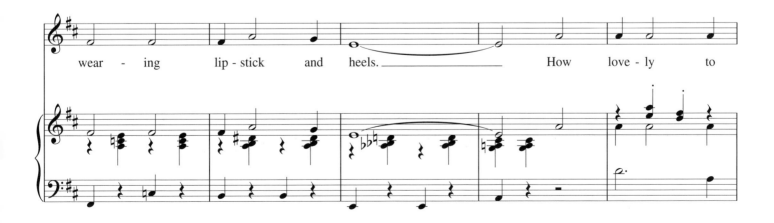

wear - ing lip-stick and heels. _____ How love-ly to

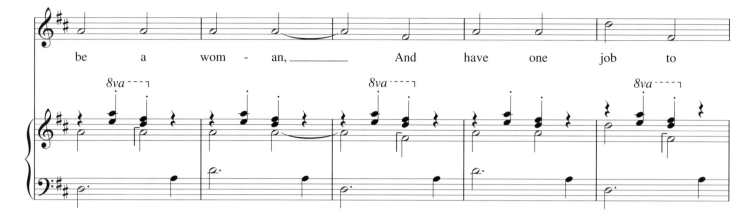

be a wom-an, _____ And have one job to

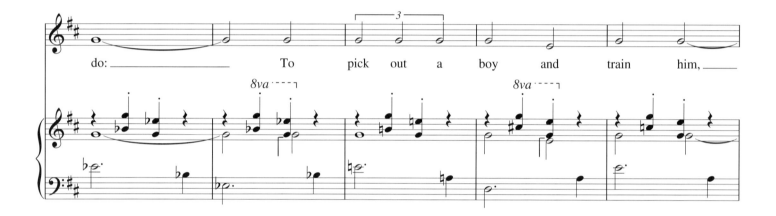

do: _____ To pick out a boy and train him, _____

____ and then when you are through, _____ You've

made him the man you want him _____ to be. _____

Life's love-ly when you're a

wom - an _____ like me! _____ How

won - der - ful to know _____ The things a wom - an

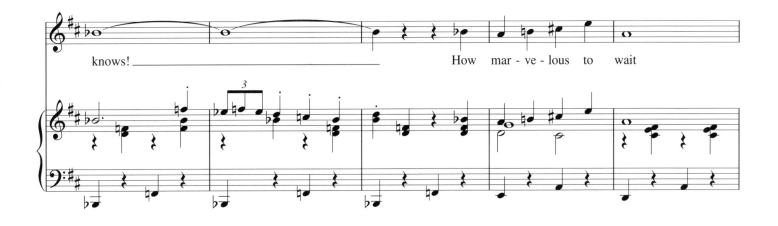

knows! _____ How mar - ve - lous to wait

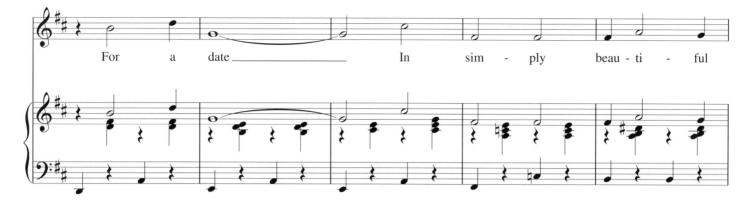

For a date _____ In sim - ply beau - ti - ful

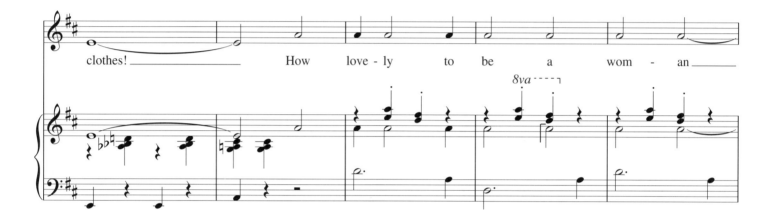

clothes! _____ How love - ly to be a wom - an _____

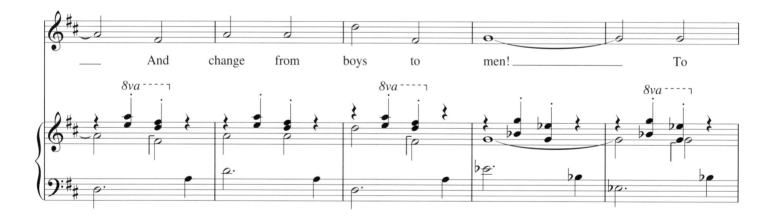

_____ And change from boys to men! _____ To

go to a fan - cy night club, _____ And stay out

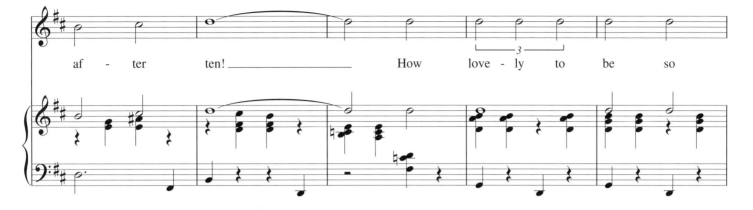

af - ter ten! _____ How love - ly to be so

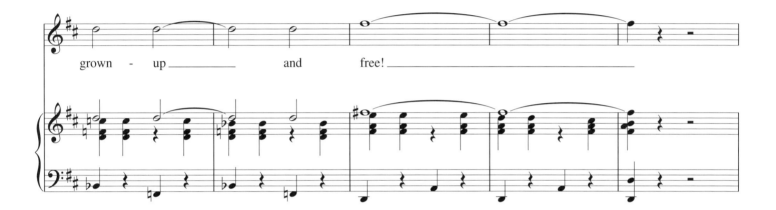

grown - up _____ and free! _____

con rubato

Life's love - ly when you're a wom - an _____

a tempo

___ like me! _____

ONE BOY
from *Bye Bye Birdie*

Lyric by LEE ADAMS
Music by CHARLES STROUSE

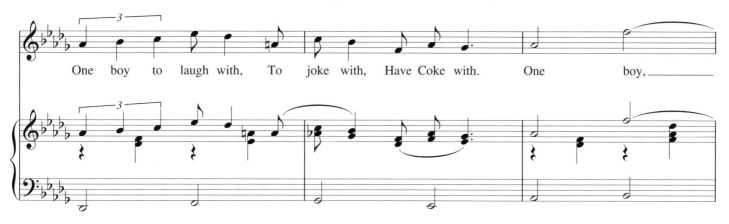

One boy to laugh with, To joke with, Have Coke with. One boy, ___

___ Not two or three. ___

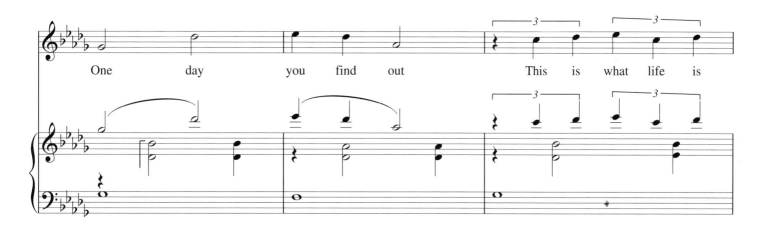

One day you find out This is what life is

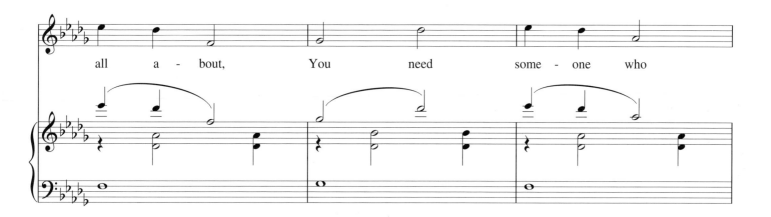

all a-bout, You need some-one who

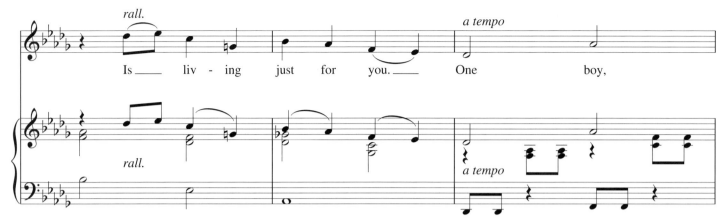

Is__ liv - ing just for you.__ One boy,

One stead - y boy, One boy to be with, For - ev - er And ev - er.

One boy, That's the way it should be,_____

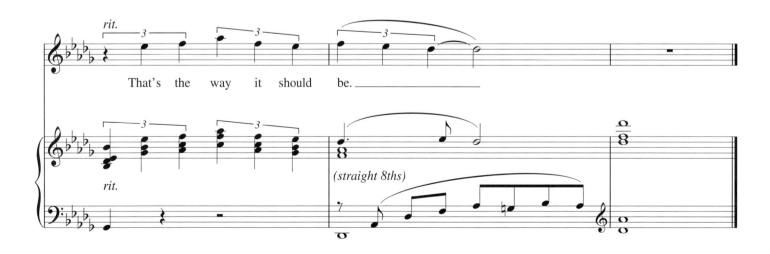

That's the way it should be._____

IT'S A MOST UNUSUAL DAY

from *A Date with Judy*

Words by HAROLD ADAMSON
Music by JIMMY McHUGH

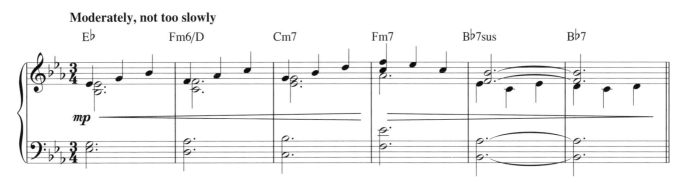

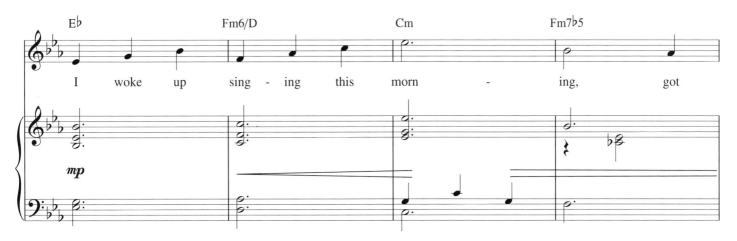

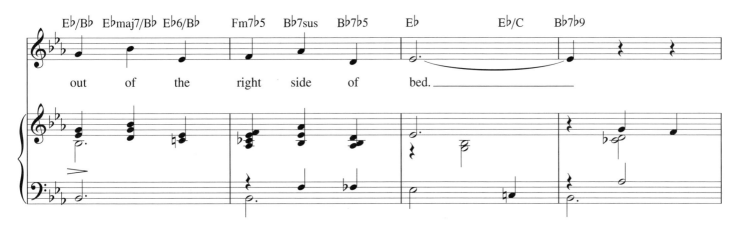

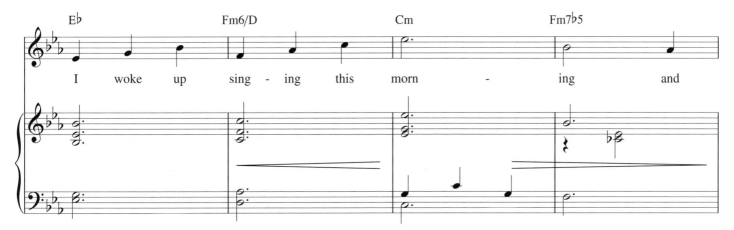

won - der - ing what was a - head._____ I

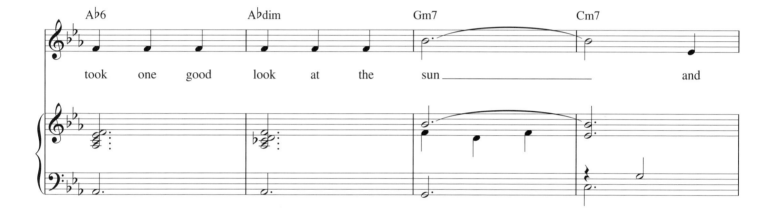

took one good look at the sun _____ and

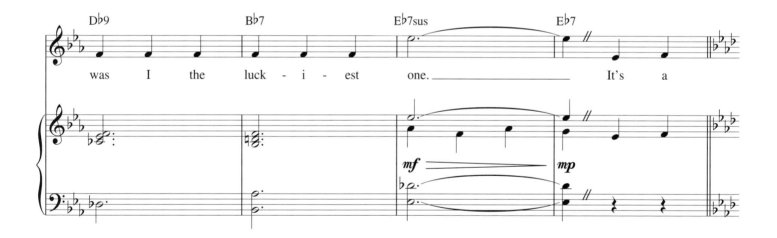

was I the luck - i - est one._____ It's a

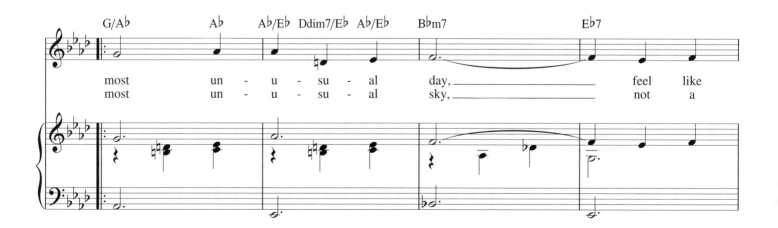

most un - u - su - al day,_____ feel like
most un - u - su - al sky,_____ not a

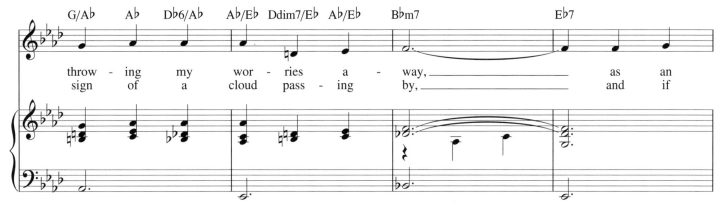

throw - ing my wor - ries a - way, _____ as an
sign of a cloud pass - ing by, _____ and if

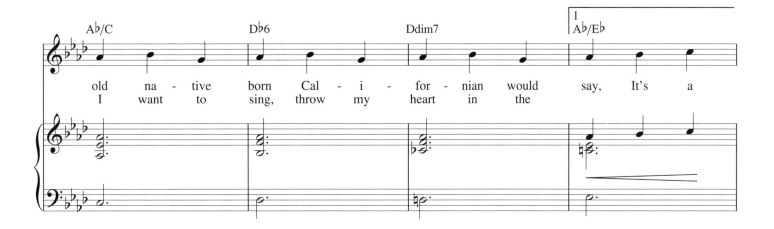

old na - tive born Cal - i - for - nian would say, It's a
I want to sing, throw my heart in the

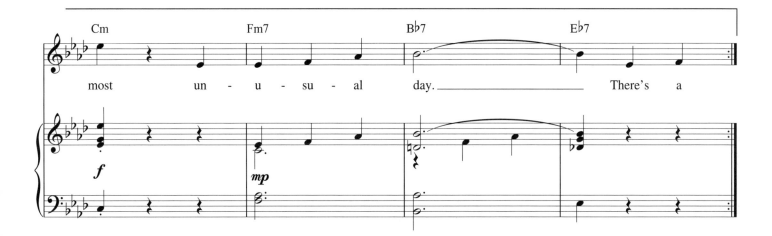

most un - u - su - al day. _____ There's a

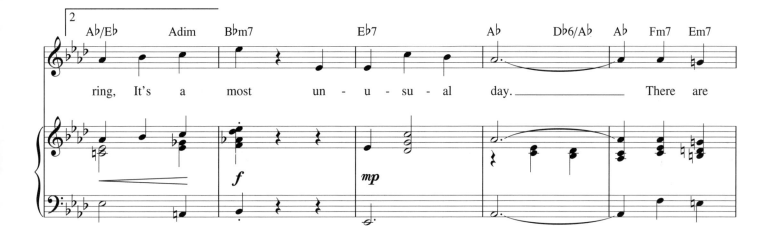

ring, It's a most un - u - su - al day. _____ There are

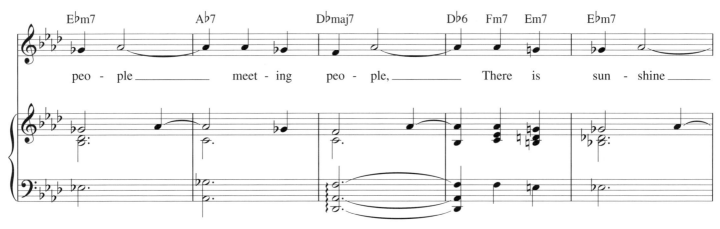

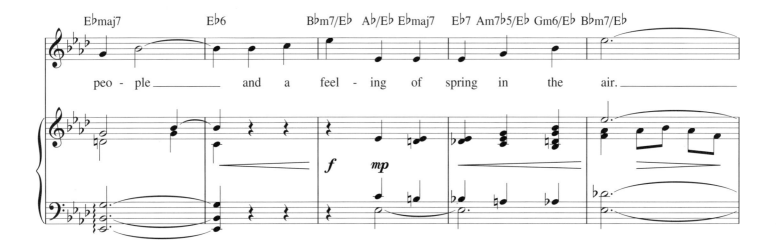

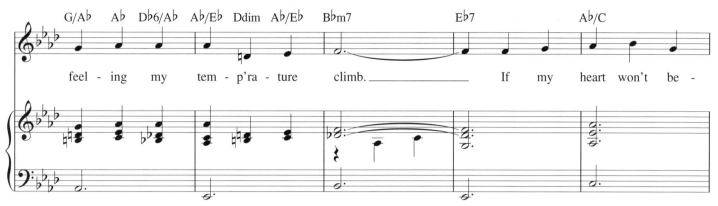

feel - ing my tem - p'ra - ture climb. _____ If my heart won't be -

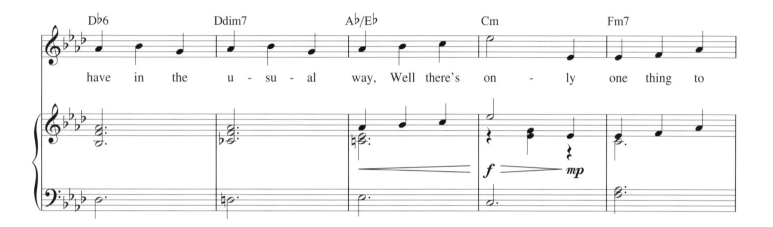

have in the u - su - al way, Well there's on - ly one thing to

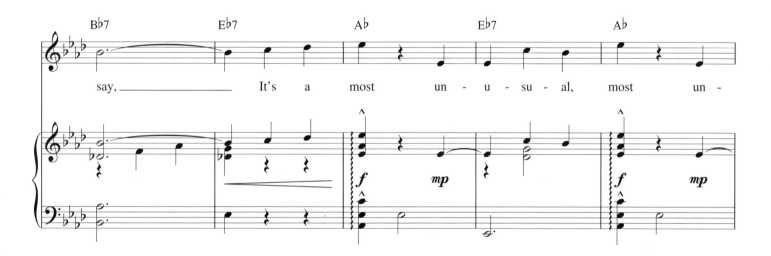

say, _____ It's a most un - u - su - al, most un -

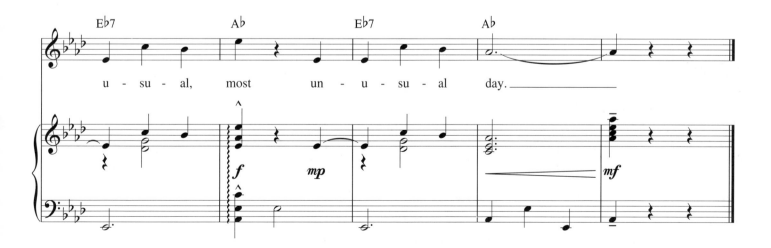

u - su - al, most un - u - su - al day. _____

A LOVELY NIGHT
from *Cinderella*

Lyrics by OSCAR HAMMERSTEIN II
Music by RICHARD RODGERS

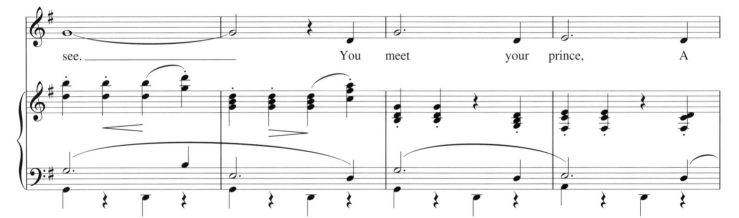

This song is an ensemble number in the show, adapted as a solo for this edition.

be! _____ The stars in a haz - y heav - en

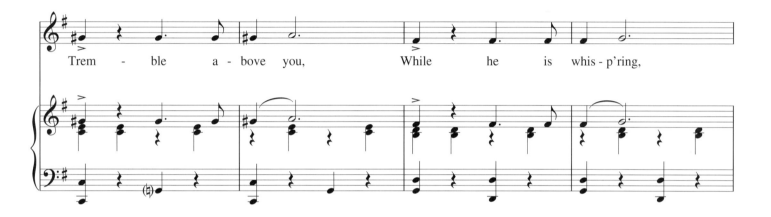

Trem - ble a - bove you, While he is whis - p'ring,

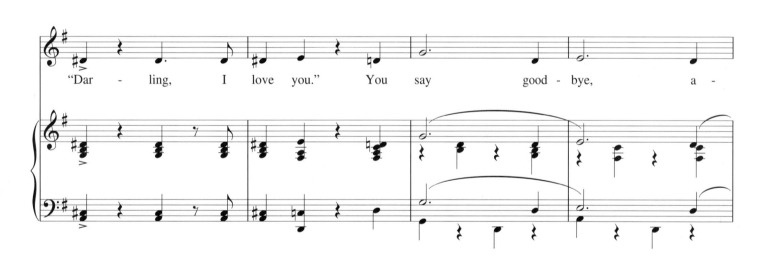

"Dar - ling, I love you." You say good - bye, a -

way you fly, But on your lips you keep a kiss;

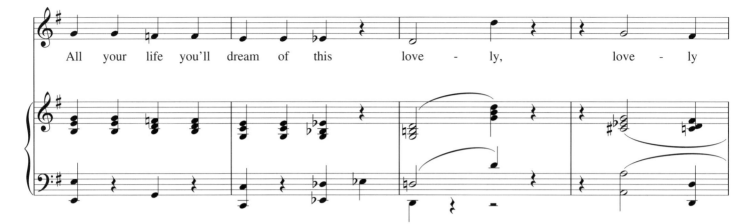

All your life you'll dream of this love - ly, love - ly

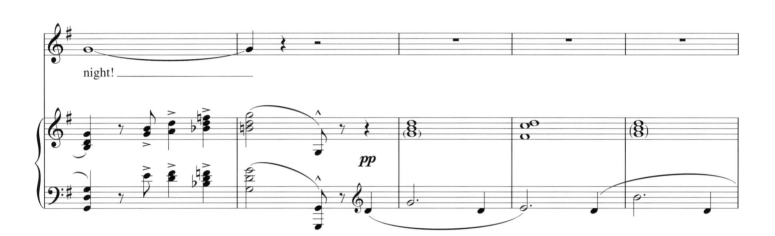

night! _____

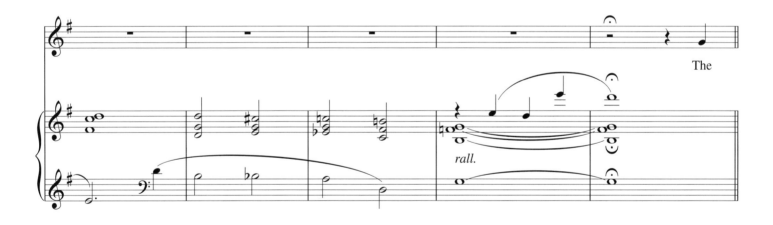

The

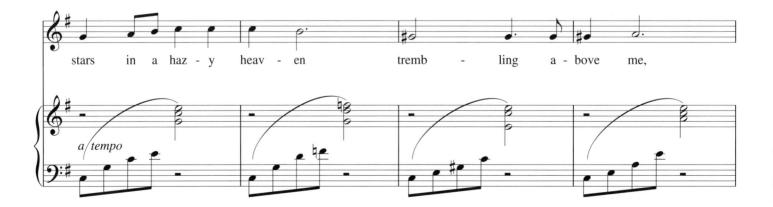

stars in a haz - y heav - en tremb - ling a - bove me,

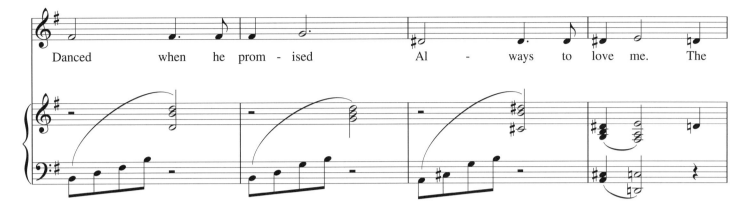

Danced when he prom - ised Al - ways to love me. The

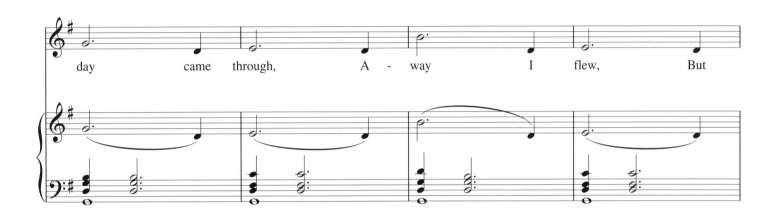

day came through, A - way I flew, But

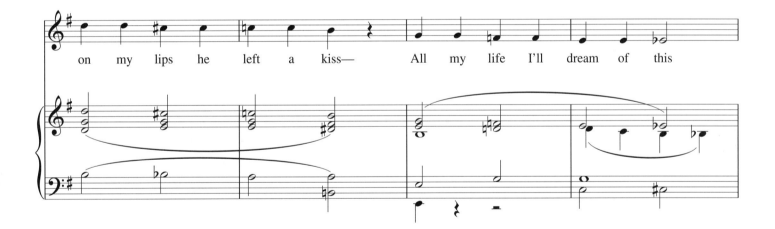

on my lips he left a kiss— All my life I'll dream of this

Love - ly, love - ly night.

rall.

NELSON
from *A Day in Hollywood/A Night in the Ukraine*

Music and Lyric by
JERRY HERMAN

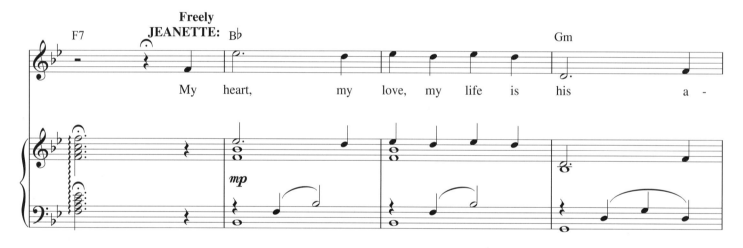

My heart, my love, my life is his a-

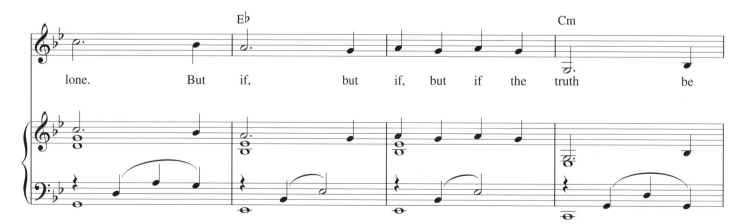

lone. But if, but if, but if the truth be

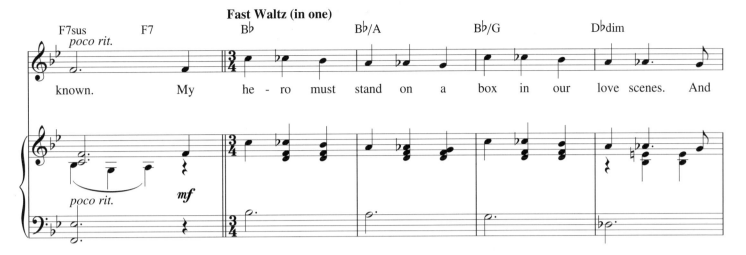

Fast Waltz (in one)

known. My he - ro must stand on a box in our love scenes. And

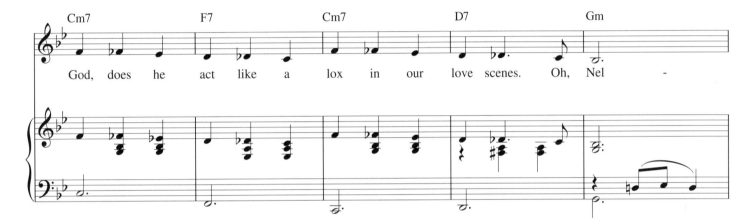

God, does he act like a lox in our love scenes. Oh, Nel -

son, what you're put - ting me through, oo oo oo oo.

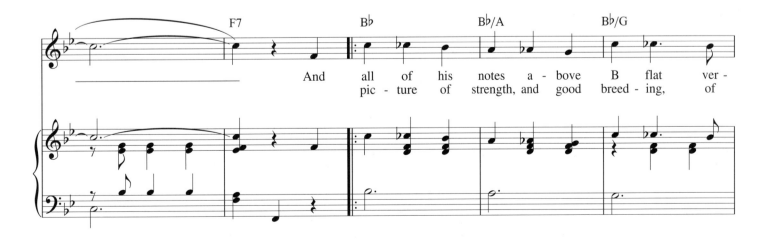

And all of his notes a - bove B flat ver-
pic - ture of strength, and good breed - ing, of

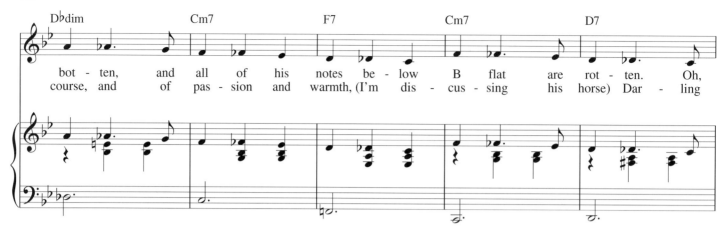

bot - ten, and all of his notes be - low B flat are rot - ten. Oh,
course, and of pas - sion and warmth, (I'm dis - cus - sing his horse) Dar - ling

Nel - son, don't call me, I'll call you, oo oo oo
Nel - son, don't call me, I'll call you, oo oo oo

oo. _____
oo. _____

His love - mak - ing casts such a
A sym - bol of vir - tue and

pall, _____ It's hard not to sleep through it all. _____
class, _____ A - mer - i - ca's sweet - hearts, my ass. _____

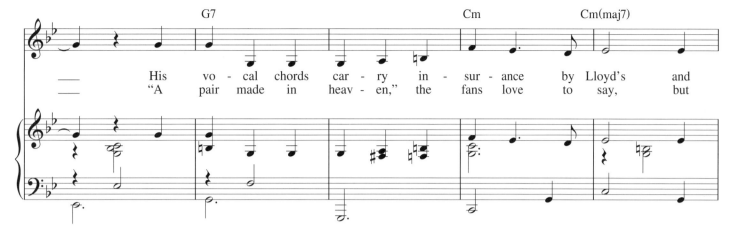

His vo-cal chords car-ry in-sur-ance by Lloyd's and
"A pair made in heav-en," the fans love to say, but

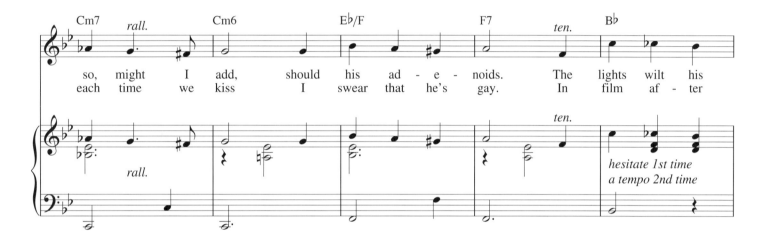

so, might I add, should his ad-e-noids. The lights wilt his
each time we kiss I swear that he's gay. In film af-ter

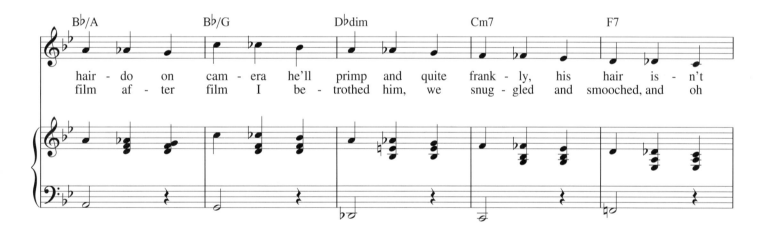

hair-do on cam-era he'll primp and quite frank-ly, his hair is-n't
film af-ter film I be-trothed him, we snug-gled and smooched, and oh

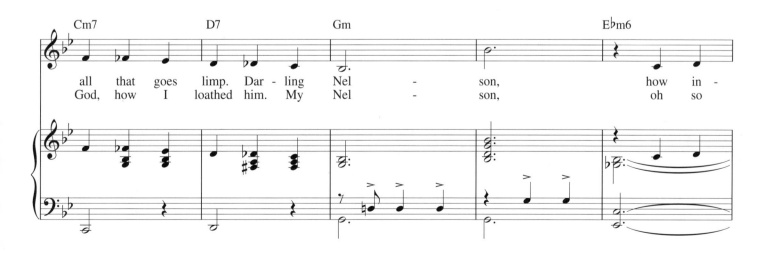

all that goes limp. Dar-ling Nel - son, how in-
God, how I loathed him. My Nel - son, oh so

I LIKE HIM
from *Drat! The Cat!*

Lyric by IRA LEVIN
Music by MILTON SCHAFER

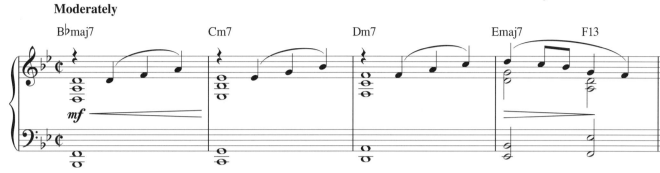

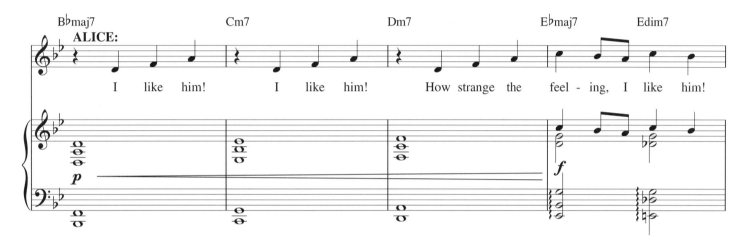

ALICE: I like him! I like him! How strange the feel-ing, I like him!

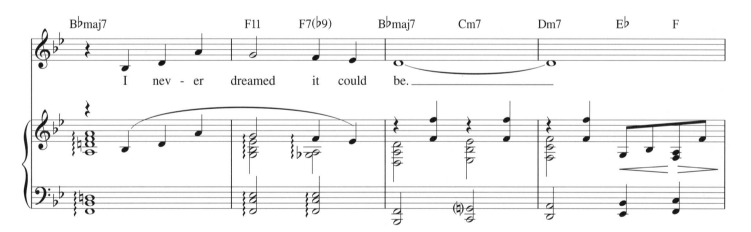

I nev-er dreamed it could be. _____

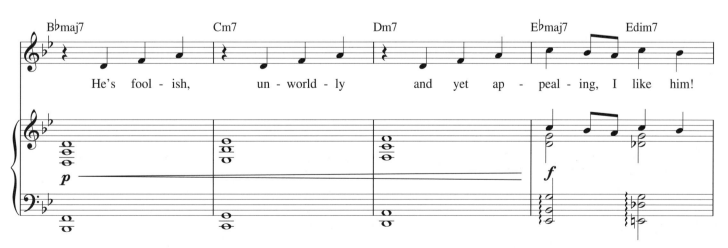

He's fool-ish, un-world-ly and yet ap-peal-ing, I like him!

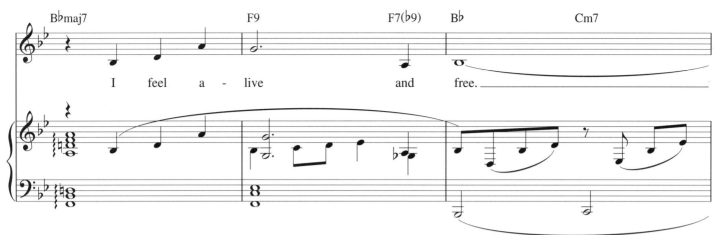

I feel a - live and free.____

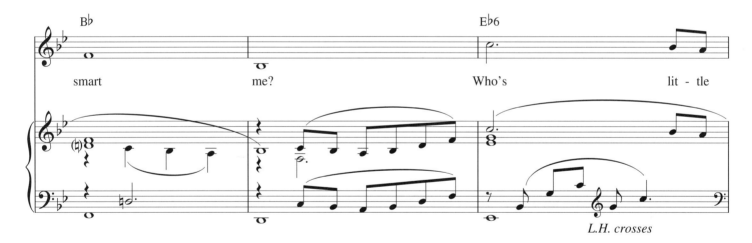

____ How did the birds and the bees out-

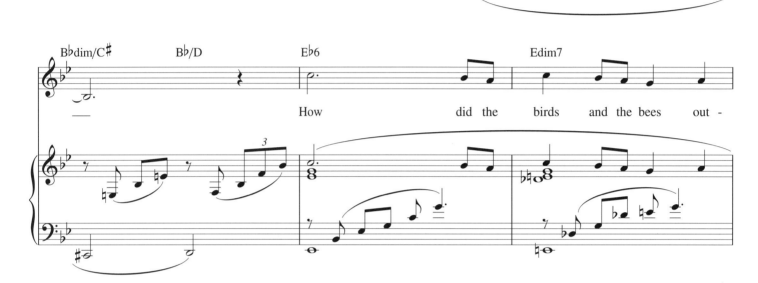

smart me? Who's lit - tle

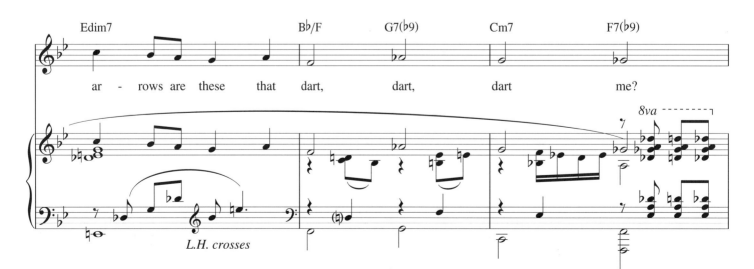

ar - rows are these that dart, dart, dart me?

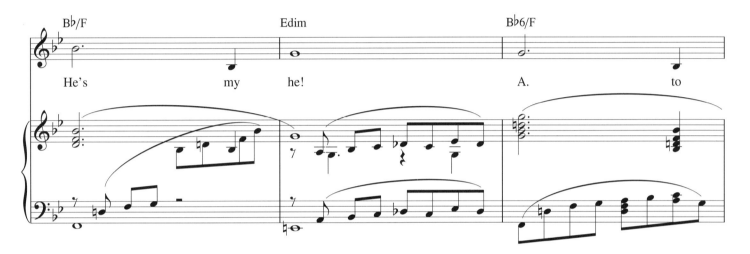

I HAVE TO TELL YOU
from *Fanny*

Words and Music by
HAROLD ROME

Appassionato e agitato

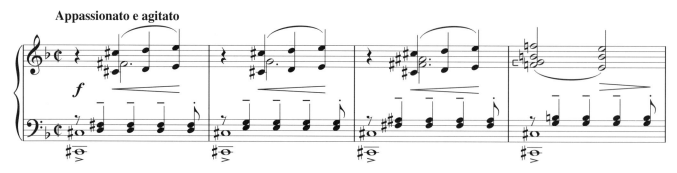

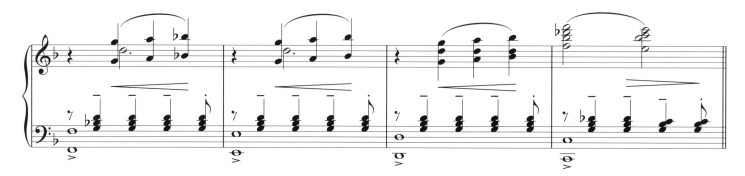

FANNY:

I have to, I have to, I have to tell you;

I have to, but I don't know where to start. ____

poco cresc.

I have to, I have to, I have to say what I'm

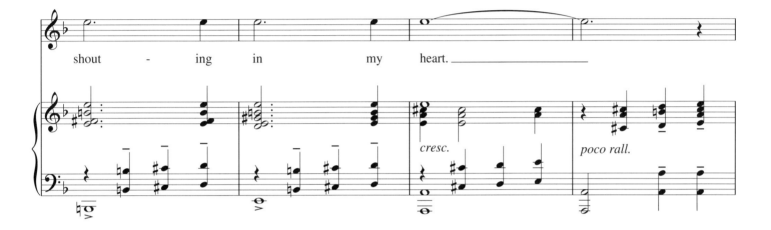

shout - ing in my heart.

cresc. *poco rall.*

Poco meno mosso

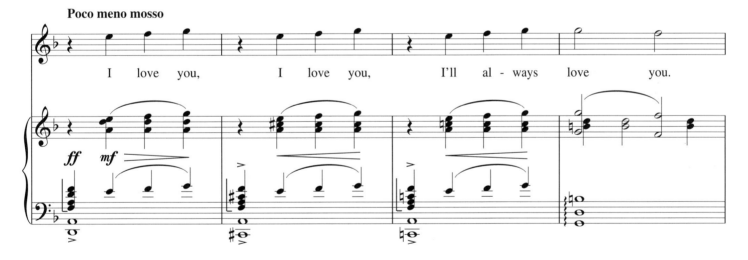

I love you, I love you, I'll al - ways love you.

ff *mf*

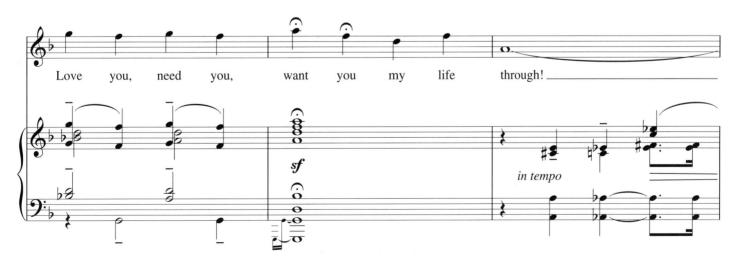

Love you, need you, want you my life through!

sf *in tempo*

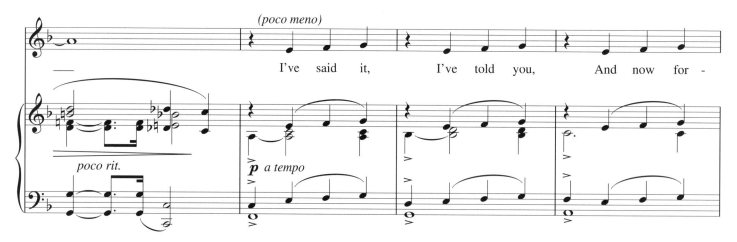

I've said it, I've told you, And now for-

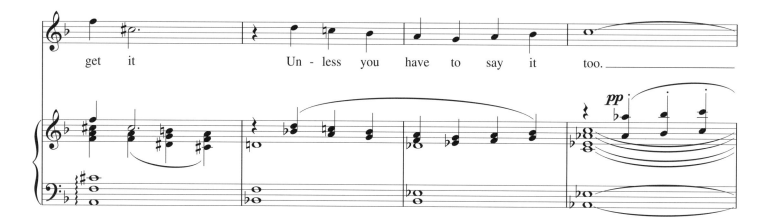

get it Un-less you have to say it too.____

May - be you do.____

LOVELY
from *A Funny Thing Happened on the Way to the Forum*

Words and Music by
STEPHEN SONDHEIM

This song is a duet for Philia and Hero in the show, adapted as a solo for this edition.

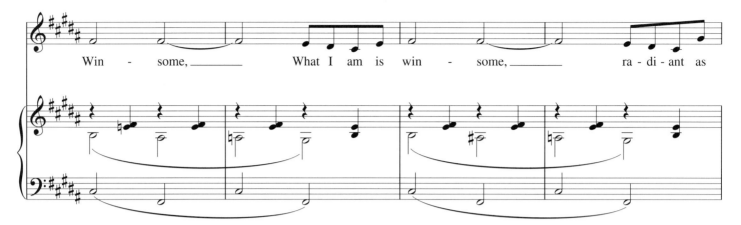

Win - some,_____ What I am is win - some,_____ ra - di - ant as

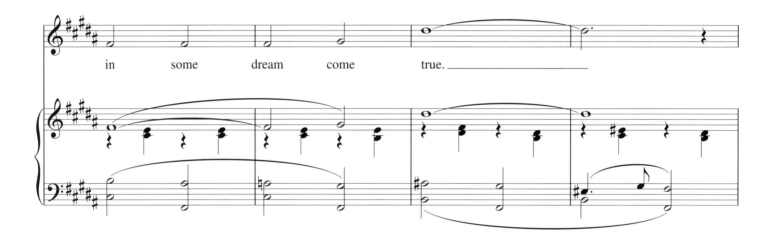

in some dream come true._____

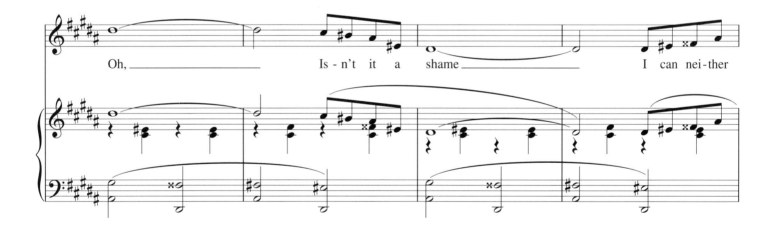

Oh,_____ Is - n't it a shame_____ I can nei - ther

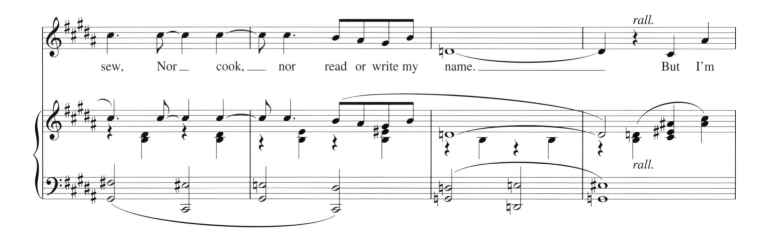

sew, Nor cook,___ nor read or write my name._____ But I'm

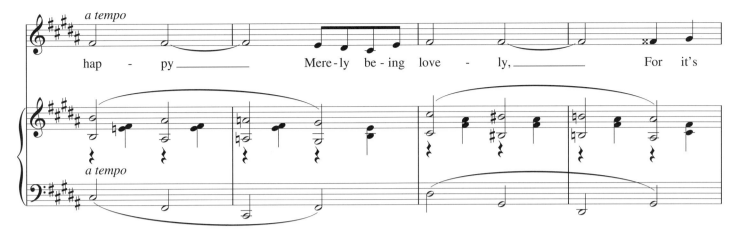

hap - py _____ Mere-ly be - ing love - ly, _____ For it's

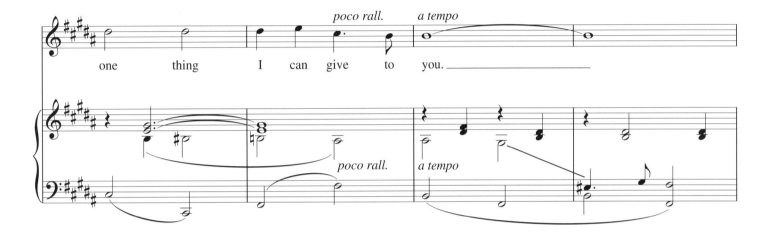

one thing I can give to you. _____

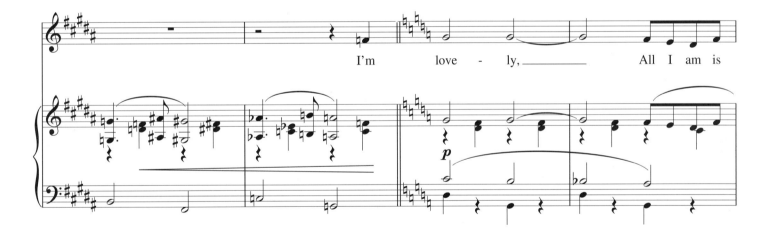

I'm love - ly, _____ All I am is

love - ly. _____ Love-ly is the one thing I can

do. _____ Win - some, _____ What I am is

win - some, _____ Ra - di - ant as in some dream come

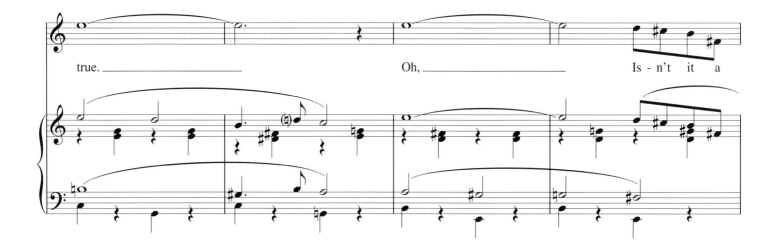

true. _____ Oh, _____ Is - n't it a

shame _____ I can nei-ther sew, Nor___ cook,___ nor read or write my

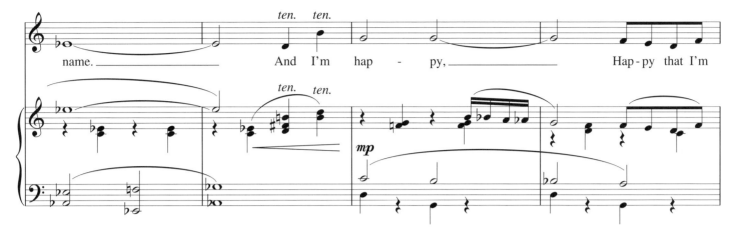

ten. ten.

name._____ And I'm hap - py,_____ Hap - py that I'm

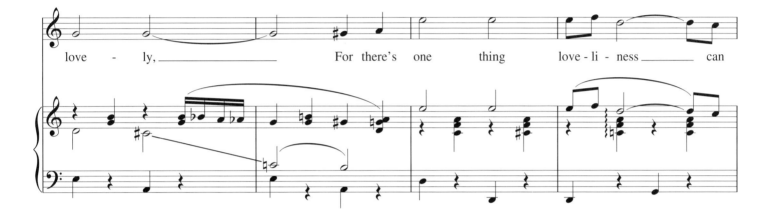

love - ly,_____ For there's one thing love - li - ness____ can

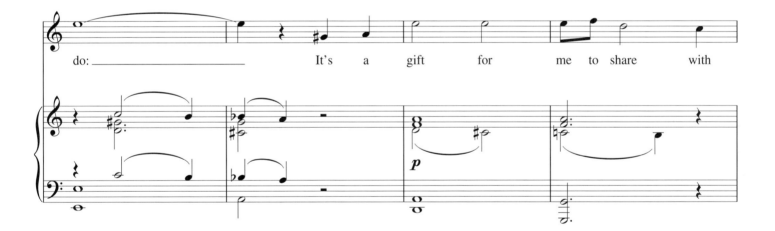

do:_____ It's a gift for me to share with

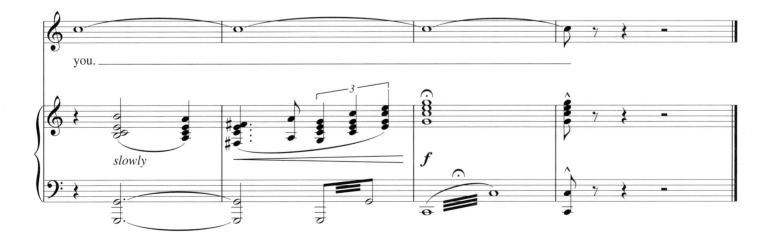

you._____

A QUIET THING

from *Flora, The Red Menace*

Words by FRED EBB
Music by JOHN KANDER

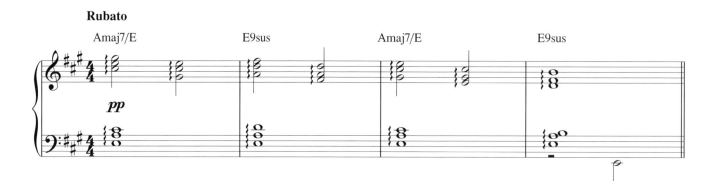

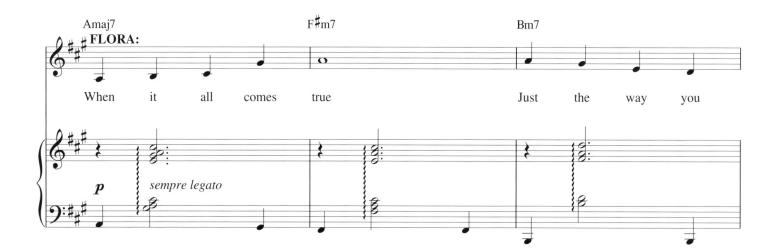

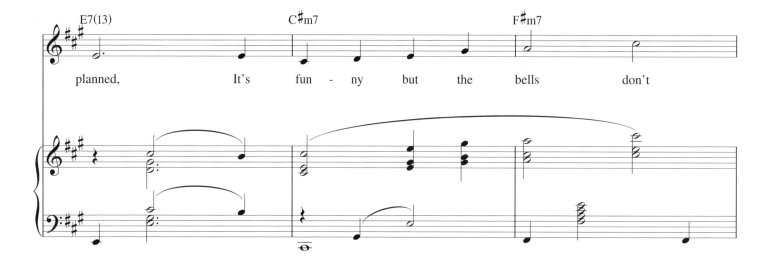

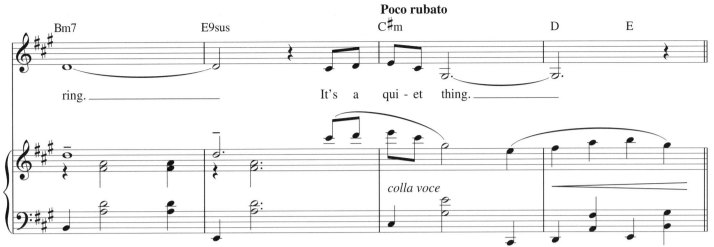

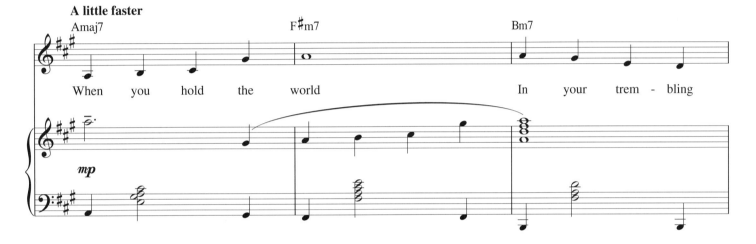

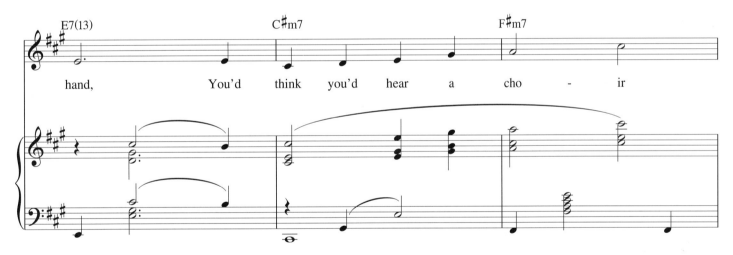

Con moto

There are no ex-plod - ing fi - re-works. Where's the roar-ing of the

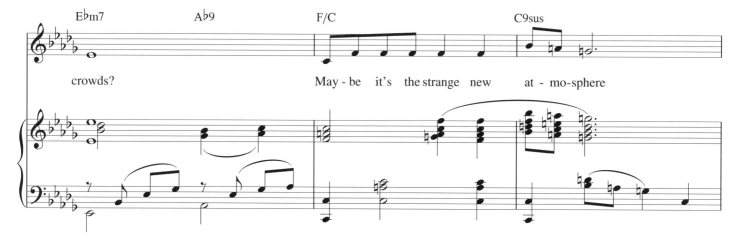

crowds? May - be it's the strange new at - mo-sphere

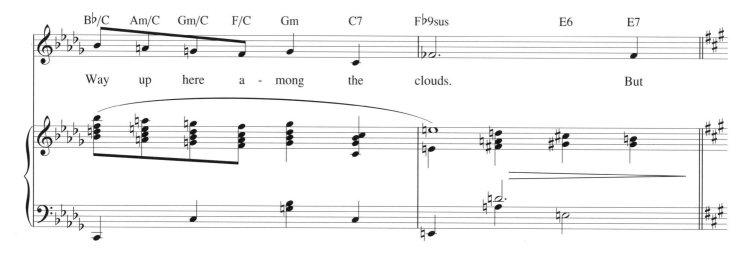

Way up here a - mong the clouds. But

Tempo I

I don't hear the drums, I don't hear the band, The

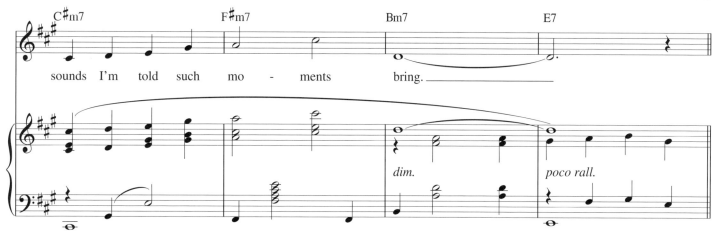

sounds I'm told such mo - ments bring.

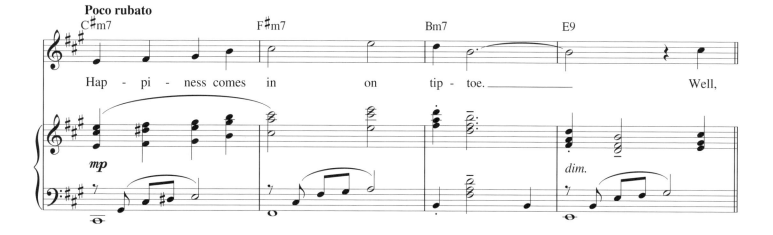

Poco rubato

Hap - pi - ness comes in on tip - toe. Well,

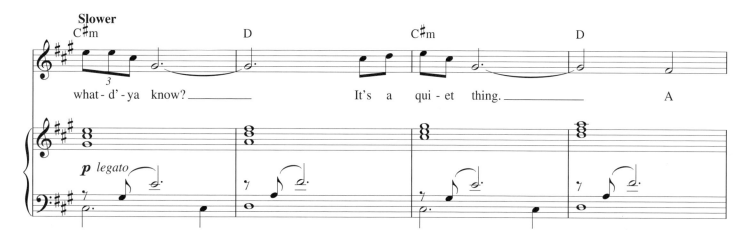

Slower

what - d' - ya know? It's a qui - et thing. A

ver - y qui - et thing.

ON THE STEPS OF THE PALACE
from *Into the Woods*

Music and Lyrics by
STEPHEN SONDHEIM

bet - ter off there where there's noth-ing to choose, so there's nothing to lose._____ So you

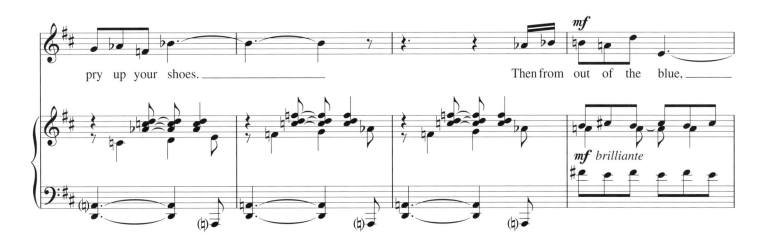

pry up your shoes._____ Then from out of the blue,_____

And with - out an - y guide,_____ You know what your de - ci - sion is,___

Which is not to de - cide. You'll just leave him a clue:

For ex - am - ple, a shoe. And then see what he'll do.

Now it's he and not you who is stuck with a shoe, In a stew, In the goo,

cresc.

And you've learned some-thing, too, Some-thing you nev-er knew, ____

mf

On the steps of the pal - ace. ____

CHILDREN WILL LISTEN

from *Into the Woods*

Music and Lyrics by
STEPHEN SONDHEIM

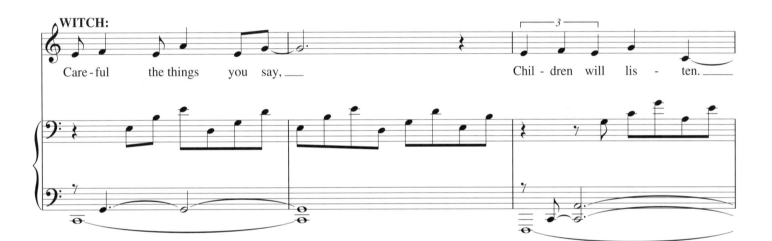

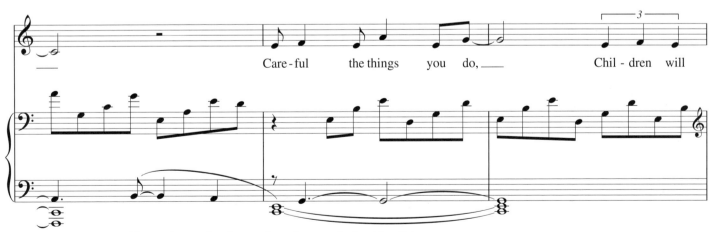

This song is an ensemble number in the show, adapted as a solo for this edition.

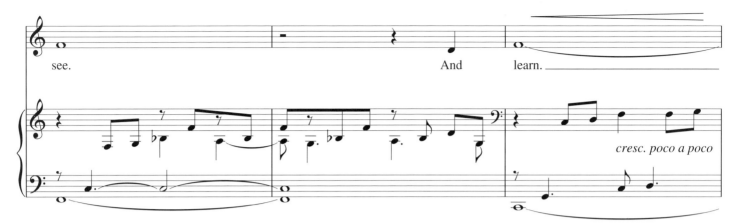

see.　　　　　　　　　　　　And　learn.

cresc. poco a poco

Chil-dren　may not　o - bey,　　　but

mp

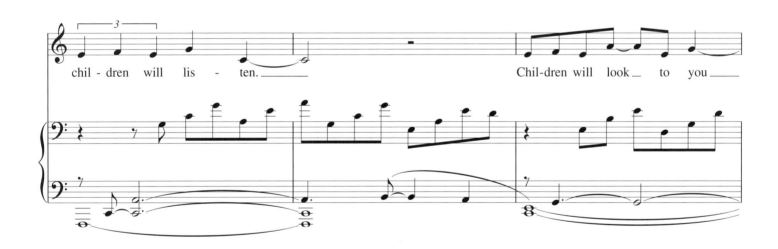

chil - dren will lis - ten.　　　Chil-dren will look＿ to　you＿

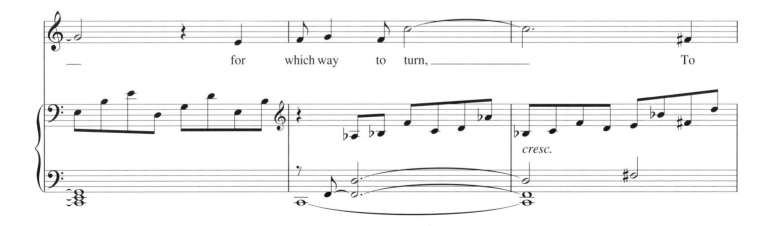

for　which way　to　turn,　　　　　　To

cresc.

Care - ful the path they take — Wish - es come true,

Not free.

cresc. poco a poco

Care - ful the spell you cast,

mf

Not just on chil - dren.

Some-times the spell _ may last _____ Past what you can see _____

And turn a - gainst you... _____

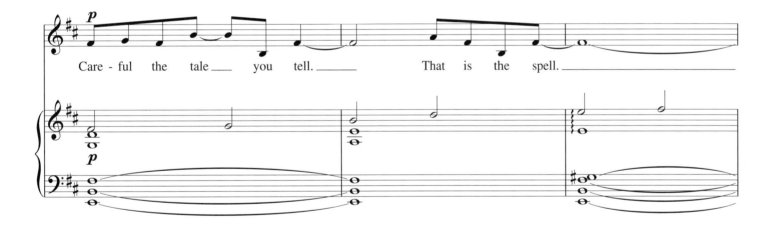

Care - ful the tale ___ you tell. _____ That is the spell. _____

Chil-dren will lis - ten...

I HAVE DREAMED
from *The King and I*

Lyrics by OSCAR HAMMERSTEIN II
Music by RICHARD RODGERS

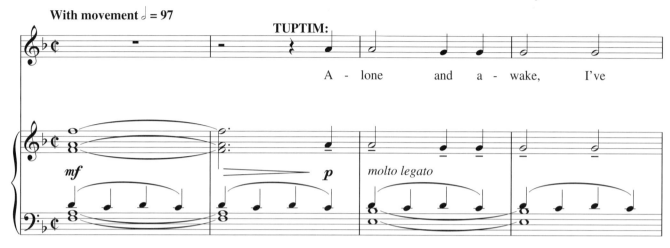

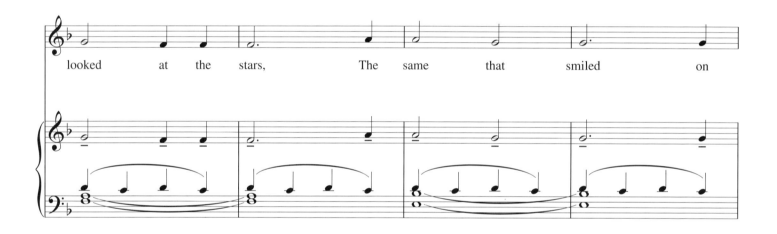

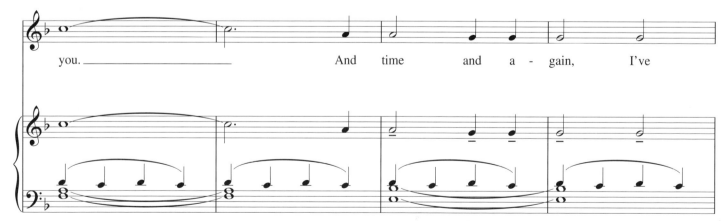

This song is a duet for Tuptim and Lun Tha in the show, adapted as a solo for this edition.

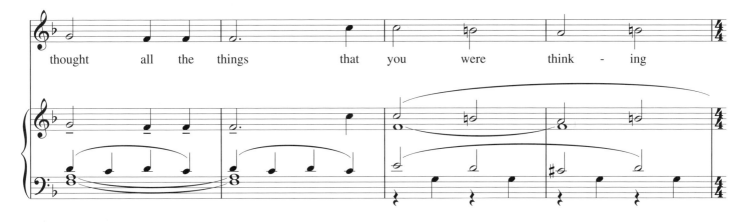

thought all the things that you were think - ing

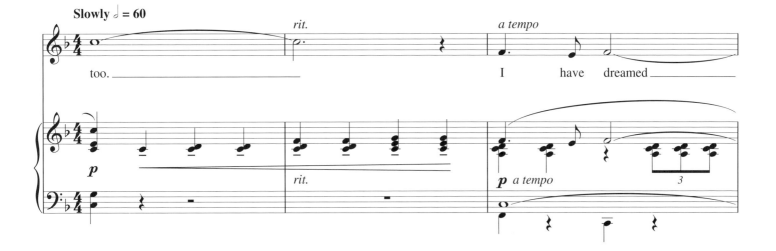

Slowly ♩ = 60
rit.
a tempo

too. I have dreamed

p
rit.
p a tempo
3

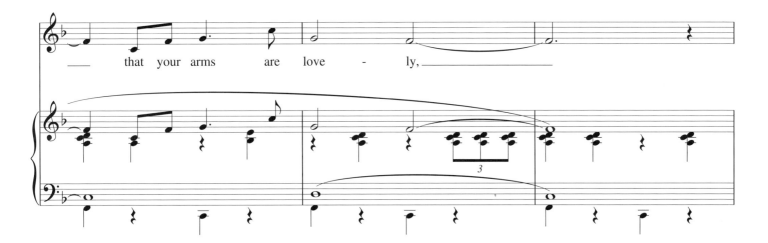

that your arms are love - ly,
3

I have dreamed what a joy you'll be.
3
3

I have dreamed _____ ev - 'ry word you'll

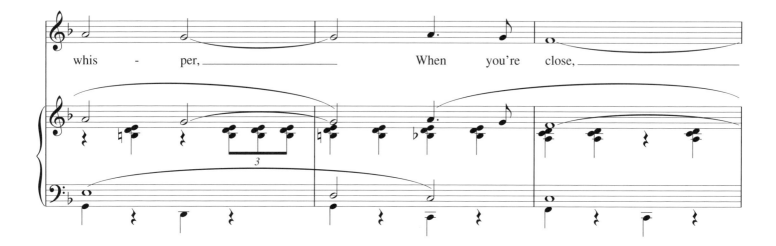

whis - per, _____ When you're close, _____

___ close to me. _____ How you look _____

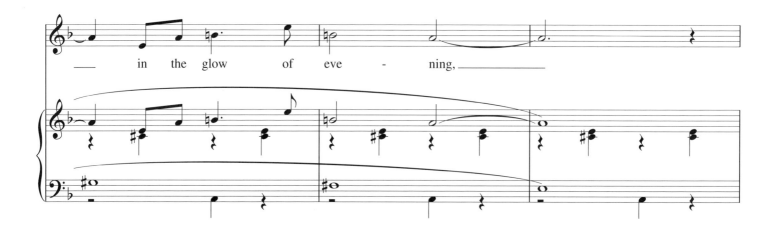

___ in the glow of eve - ning, _____

I have dreamed_____ and en - joyed the view._____

In these dreams I've loved you so That by now I think I

know What it's like to be loved by you,_____

I will love be - ing loved by you.

WE KISS IN A SHADOW
from *The King and I*

Lyrics by OSCAR HAMMERSTEIN II
Music by RICHARD RODGERS

This song is a duet for Lun Tha and Tuptim, adapted as a solo for this edition.

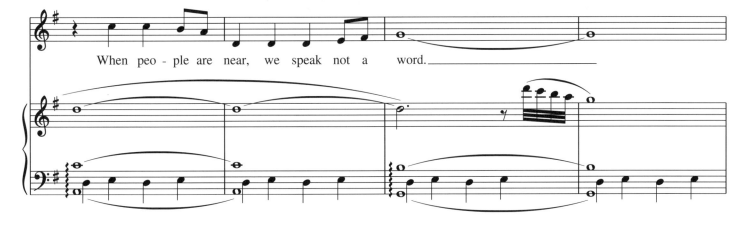

When peo - ple are near, we speak not a word.

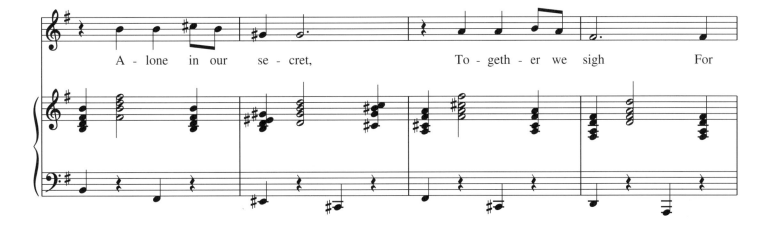

A - lone in our se - cret, To - geth - er we sigh For

one smil - ing day to be free,

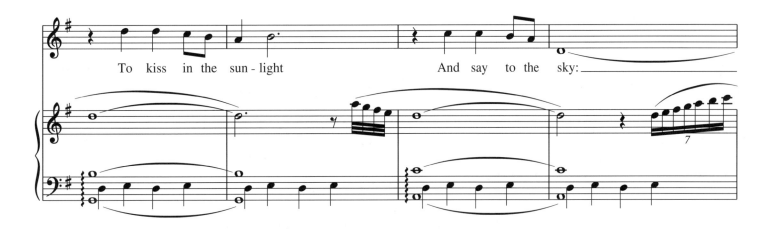

To kiss in the sun - light And say to the sky:

Be - hold and be - lieve what you see! Be -

hold how my lov - er loves me!

A - lone in our se - cret, To - geth - er we sigh For

one smil - ing day to be free,

To kiss in the sun - light

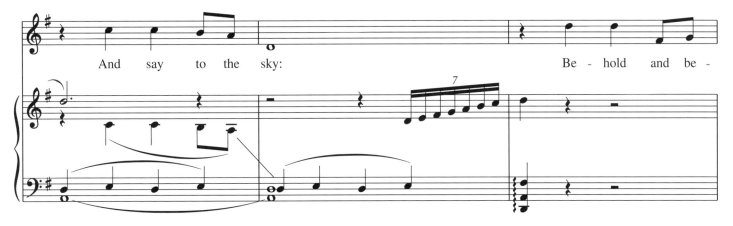

And say to the sky: Be - hold and be -

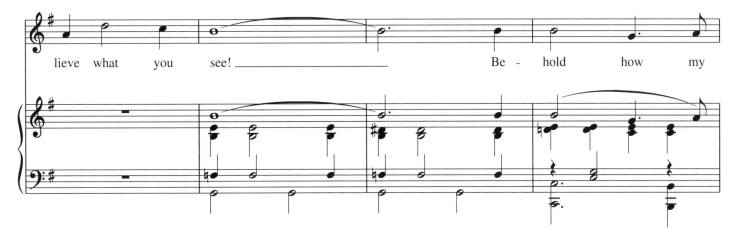

lieve what you see! _____ Be - hold how my

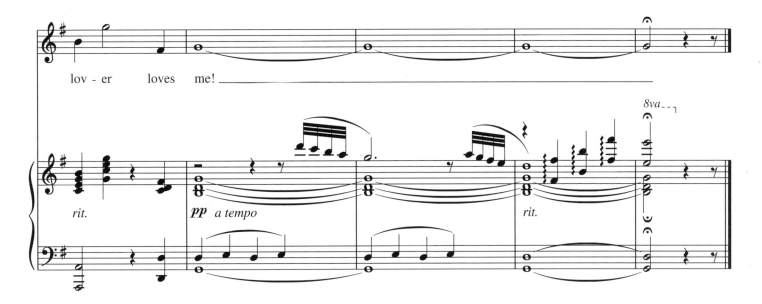

lov - er loves me! _____

rit.   *pp* *a tempo*   rit.

THE LIGHT IN THE PIAZZA

from *The Light in the Piazza*

Words and Music by
ADAM GUETTEL

Con moto (in 2)

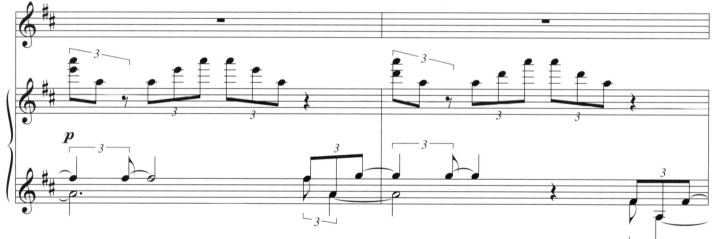

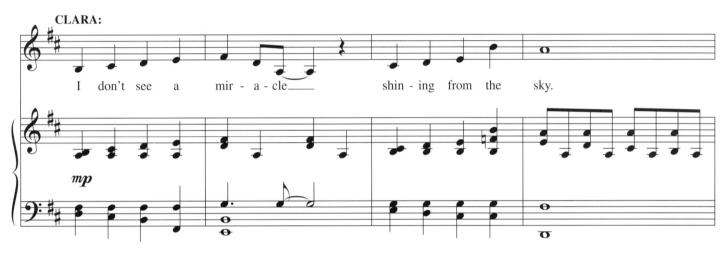

CLARA:

I don't see a mir - a - cle___ shin - ing from the sky.

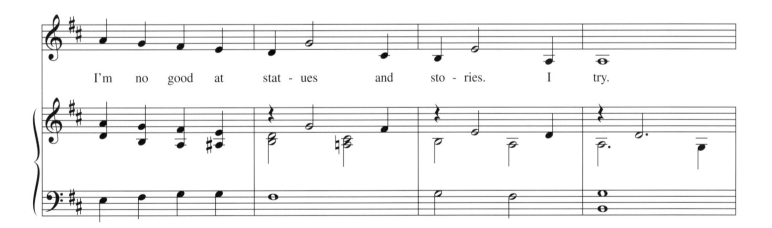

I'm no good at stat - ues and sto - ries. I try.

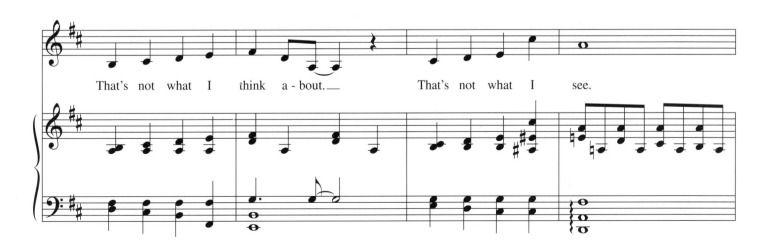

That's not what I think a - bout.___ That's not what I see.

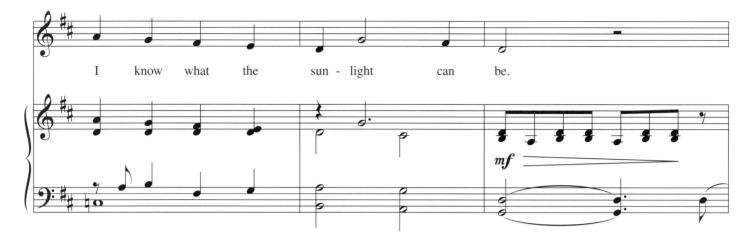

I know what the sun - light can be.

The light... The light in the piaz - za.

Ti - ny sweet,_____ and then it grows,_____ and then it fills_____ the

air.

Who knows what you call it. I don't care!

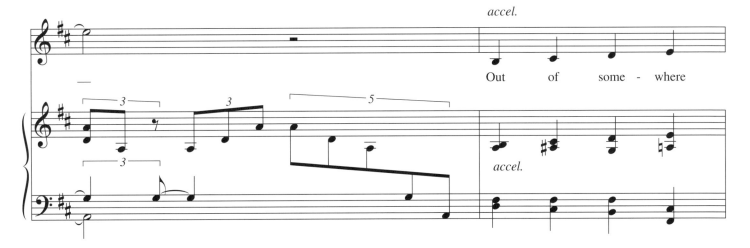

accel.

Out of some - where

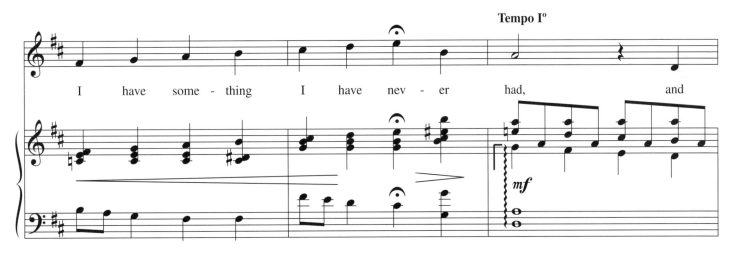

Tempo I°

I have some - thing I have nev - er had, and

sad is hap - py. That's all I see.

The light in the piaz - za.

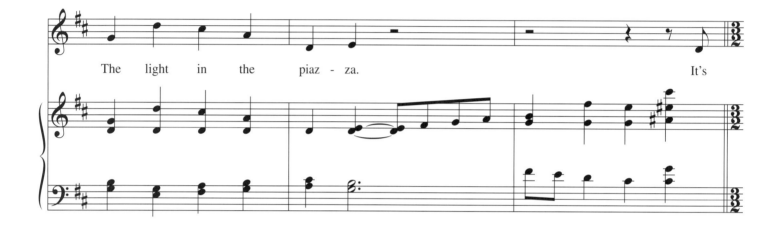

The light in the piaz - za. It's

rush - ing up.___ It's pour - ing out.___ It's fly - ing through___ the

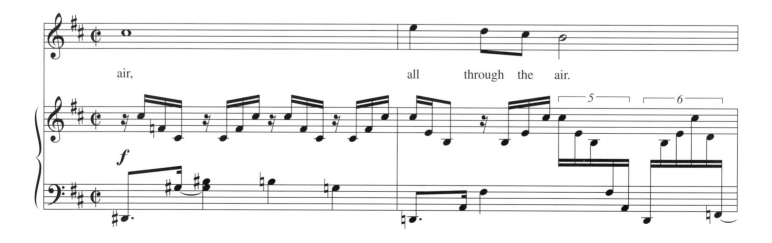

air, all through the air.

Who knows what you call it. But it's there!_____

____ It is there!_____

accel.

All I see is, all I want is tear - ing from in -

ff   *sub.* *mp*

Tempo Iº

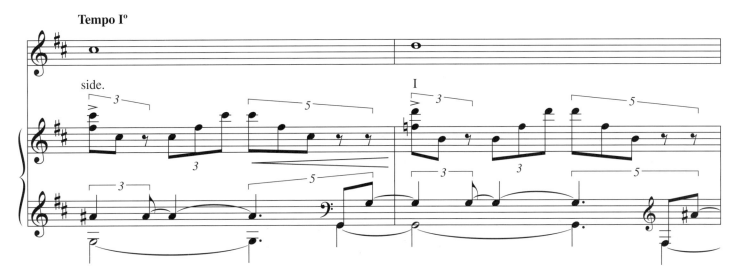

side.   I

see   it!

Now   I

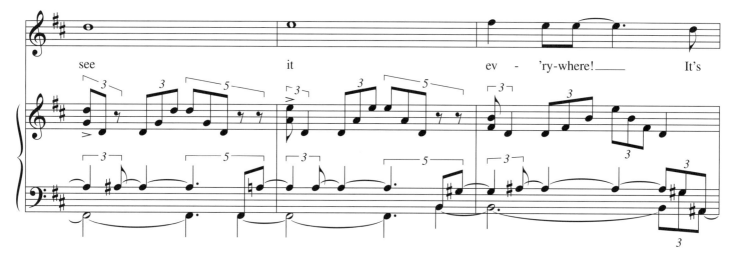

see   it   ev - 'ry-where!_____   It's

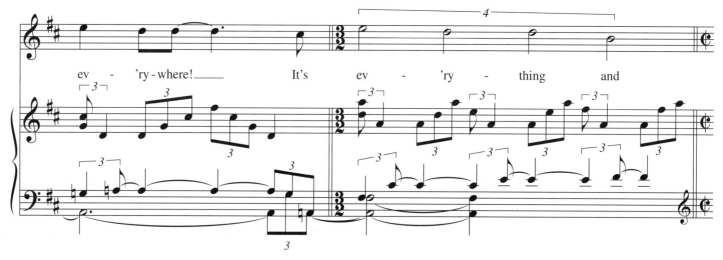

ev - 'ry-where!_____   It's   ev - 'ry - thing   and

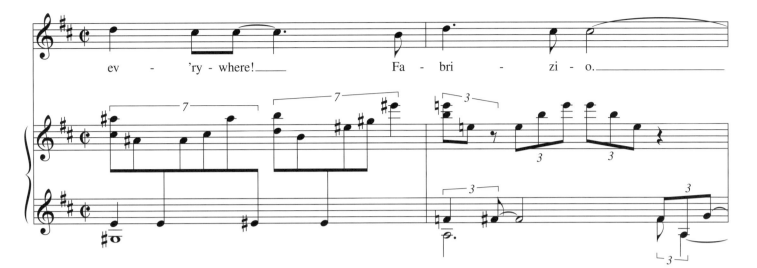

ev - 'ry - where!_____ Fa - bri - zi - o._____

The light in the

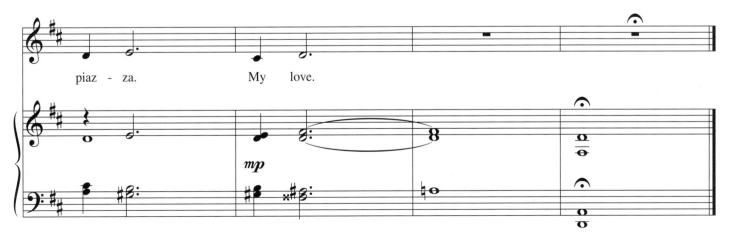

piaz - za. My love.

WHAT DOES HE WANT OF ME

from *Man of La Mancha*

Lyric by JOE DARION
Music by MITCH LEIGH

THE SONG THAT GOES LIKE THIS

from *Monty Python's Spamalot*

Lyrics by ERIC IDLE
Music by JOHN DU PREZ and ERIC IDLE

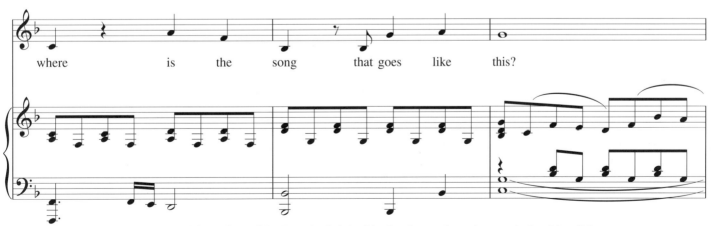

This song is a duet for the Lady of the Lake and Sir Dennis Galahad in the show, adapted as a solo for this edition.

A sen-ti-men-tal song that casts a mag-ic spell. They

all will hum a-long. We'll o - ver - act like hell. Oh, this is the

song that goes like this.

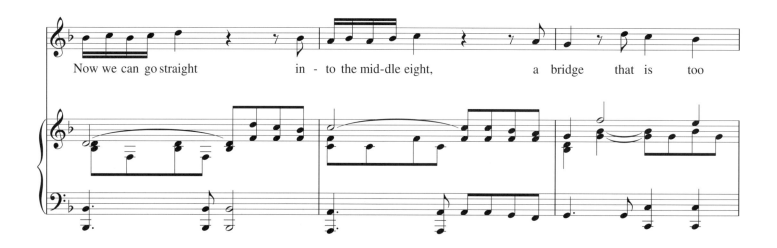

Now we can go straight in - to the mid-dle eight, a bridge that is too

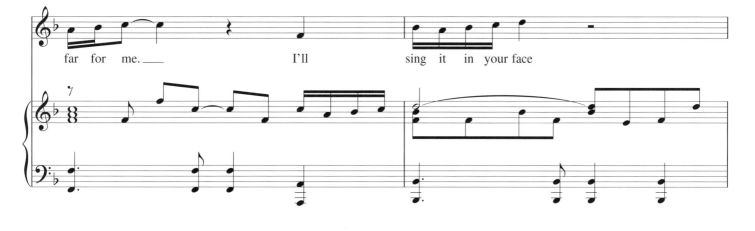

far for me. _____   I'll   sing it in your face

while we both em - brace,   and then   we change   the key! _____

Now we're in - to E.   That's aw-fully high for me   But

ev-'ry-one can see   we should have stayed in D.   For this   is   our

song　that goes　like　this. _____　I

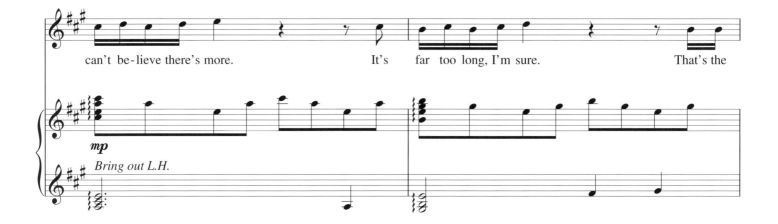

can't be-lieve there's more.　　It's　far　too long, I'm sure.　　That's the

troub-le　with this song,　　it goes　on　and　on　and　on.　For

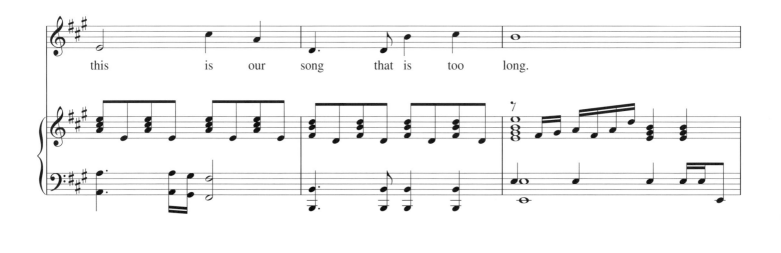

this　　is　our　song　that is　too　long.

We'll be sing-ing this 'til dawn. You'll

wish that you weren't born. Let's for - get this damn re - frain be -

fore we go in - sane. The song al - ways ends like

this!

THE SONG IS YOU
from *Music in the Air*

Lyrics by OSCAR HAMMERSTEIN II
Music by JEROME KERN

Andantino semplice

SIEGLINDE:

I hear mu-sic when I look at you, _____ A beau-ti-ful theme of ev-'ry dream I ev-er

knew, _____ Down deep in my heart, _____ I hear it play, _____ I feel it

start, _____ Then melt a - way.

I hear mu-sic when I touch your

side of me,___ Why can't I let it go,___ Why can't I let you know,___ Why can't I

let you know the song my heart would sing,___ That beau-ti-ful

rhap-so-dy of love and youth and spring,___ The mu-sic is sweet,___ The words are

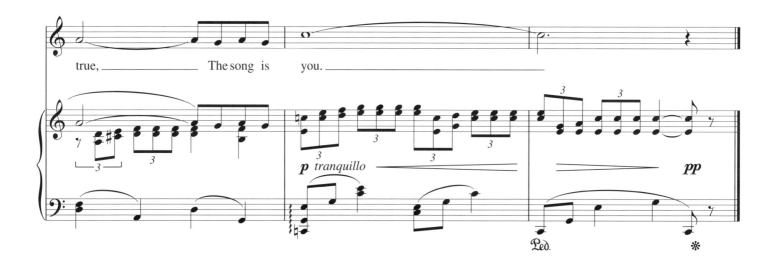

true,___ The song is you.___

MIGRATORY V
from *Myths and Hymns*

Music and Lyrics by
ADAM GUETTEL

Contemplative (♩. = 72)

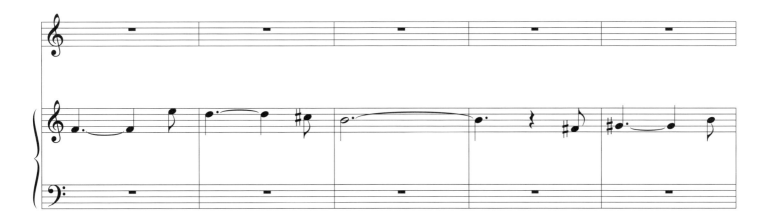

We

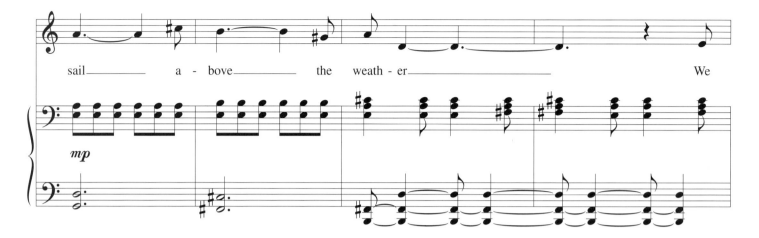

sail_____ a - bove_____ the weath - er_____ We

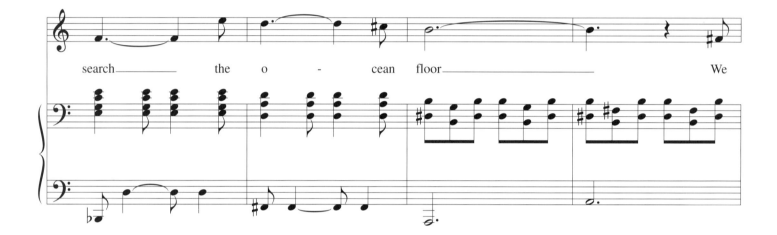

search_____ the o - cean floor_____ We

riv - al our_____ cre - a - tion_____ still

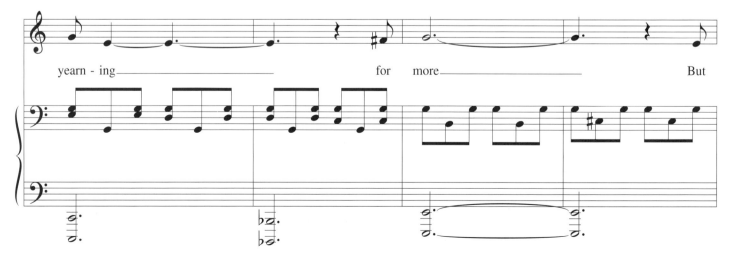

yearn - ing_____ for more_____ But

can _____ we fly _____ to - geth - er _____ a

mi - gra - tor - y V _____ How

won - der - ful _____ if that's _____ what God _____ could

see _____ A sin - gle voice in whis - pered prayer can on - ly

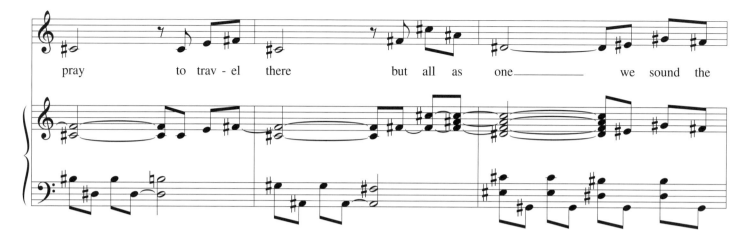

pray to trav-el there but all as one_____ we sound the

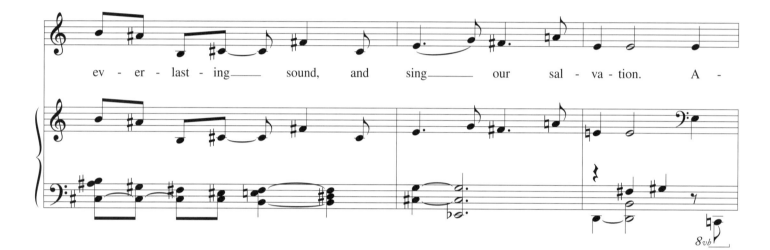

ev-er-last-ing_____ sound, and sing_____ our sal-va-tion. A-

loft and in for-ma-tion_____ a mi-gra-

tor - y V_____ How won - der - ful if_____

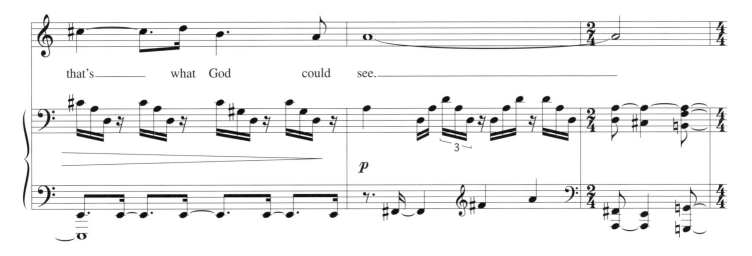

that's_____ what God could see._____

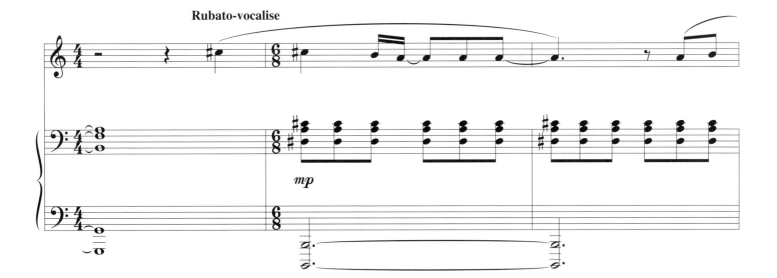

Rubato-vocalise

LOVER, COME BACK TO ME
from *The New Moon*

Lyrics by OSCAR HAMMERSTEIN II
Music by SIGMUND ROMBERG

LOVE, DON'T TURN AWAY
from *110 In the Shade*

Words by TOM JONES
Music by HARVEY SCHMIDT

do for you. _____ I have so man - y things saved up to

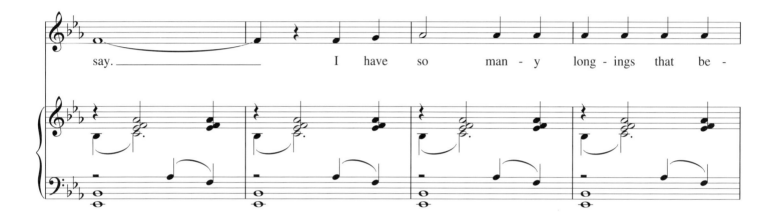

say. _____ I have so man - y long - ings that be -

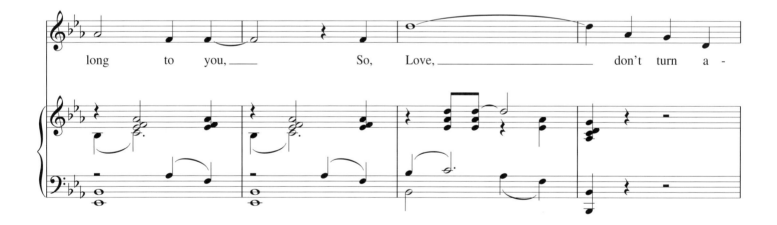

long to you, ____ So, Love, _____ don't turn a -

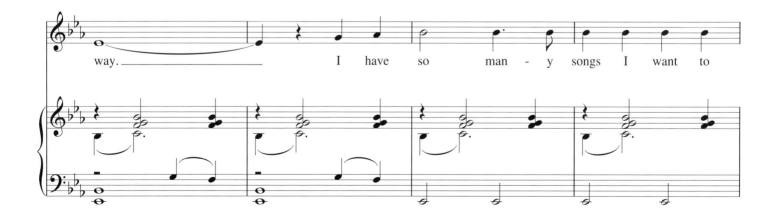

way. _____ I have so man - y songs I want to

sing to you. _____ I have so man - y smiles that I could

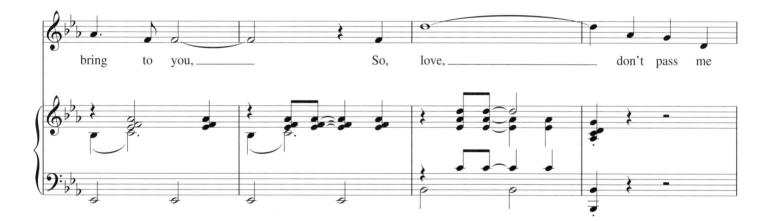

cry. _____ I have so man - y kiss - es I could

bring to you, _____ So, love, _____ don't pass me

by. _____ I can't of - fer you lots of fan - cy things To

make you come and stay. But I could wash your socks and mend your coat and

cook you lots of good things ev - 'ry day. So, Love, _____ if you're look - ing for a

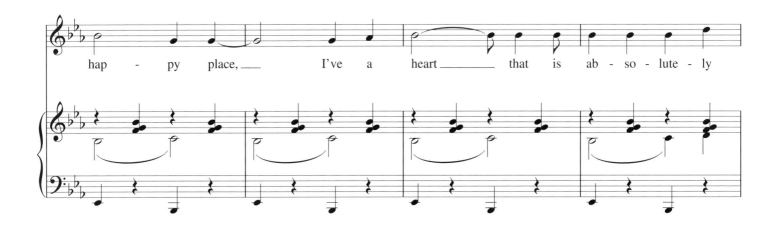

hap - py place, _____ I've a heart _____ that is ab - so - lute - ly

free! _____ O - pen arms _____ that are ach - ing for their

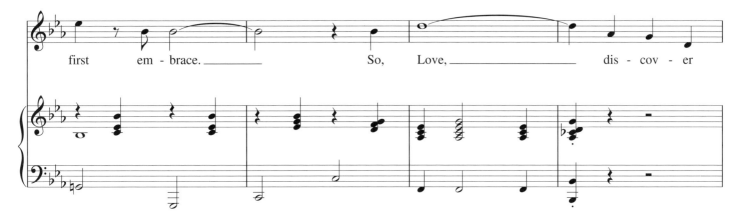

first em - brace. So, Love, dis - cov - er

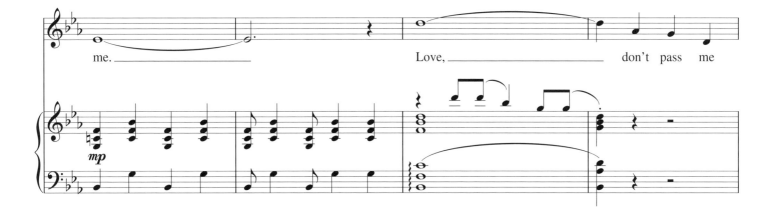

me. Love, don't pass me

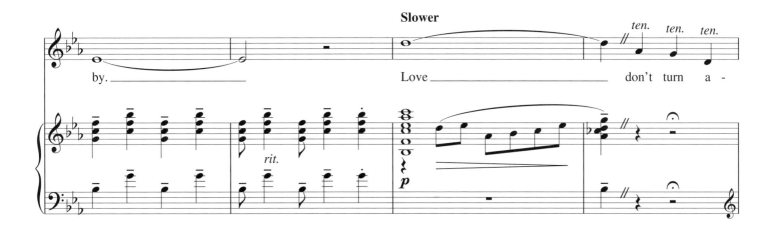

Slower

ten. *ten.* *ten.*

by. Love don't turn a -

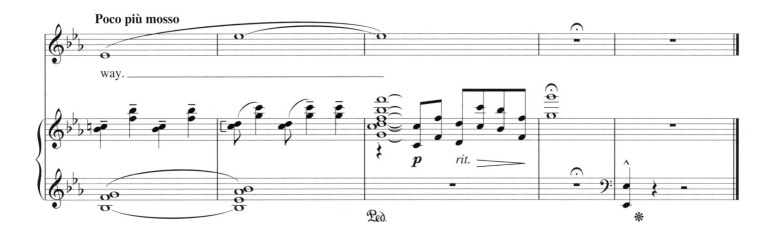

Poco più mosso

way.

Ped. *✻*

SPEAK LOW
from the Musical Production *One Touch of Venus*

Words by OGDEN NASH
Music by KURT WEILL

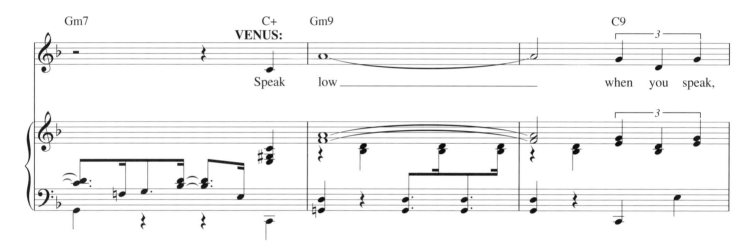

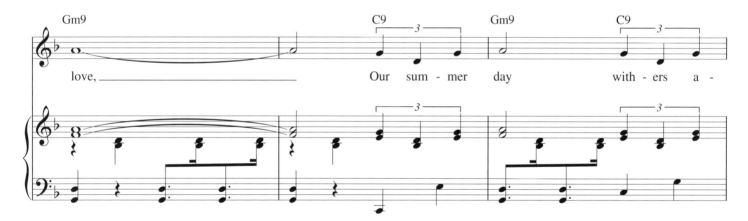

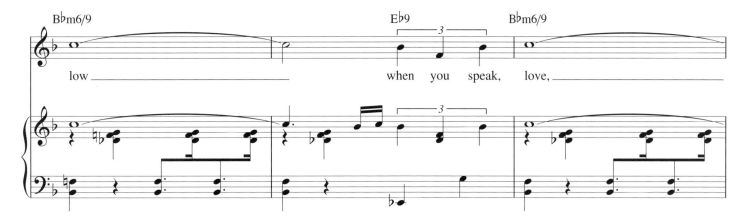

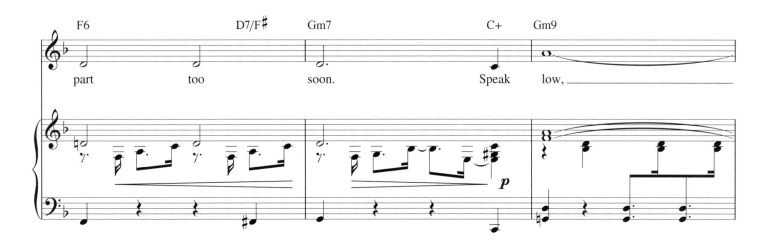

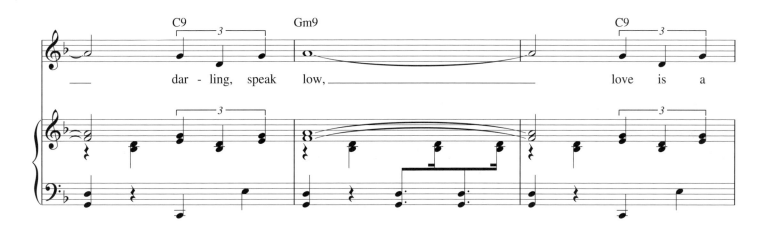

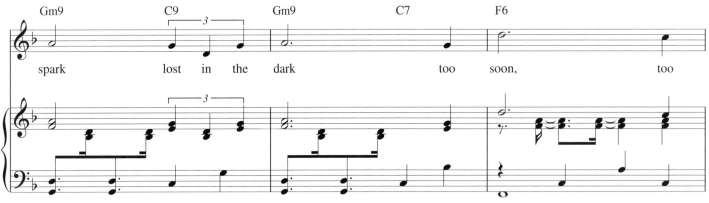

spark lost in the dark too soon, too

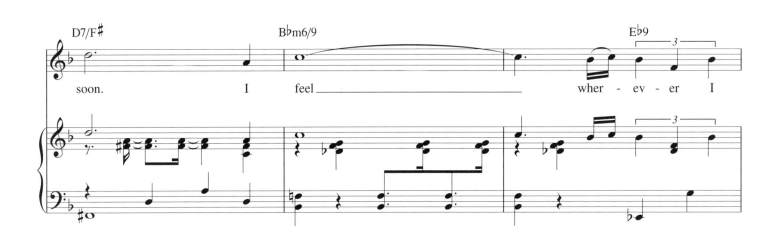

soon. I feel _____ wher - ev - er I

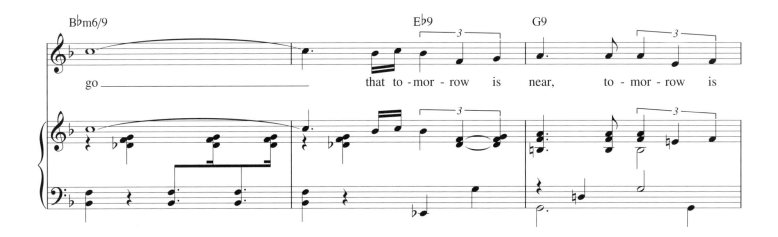

go _____ that to - mor - row is near, to - mor - row is

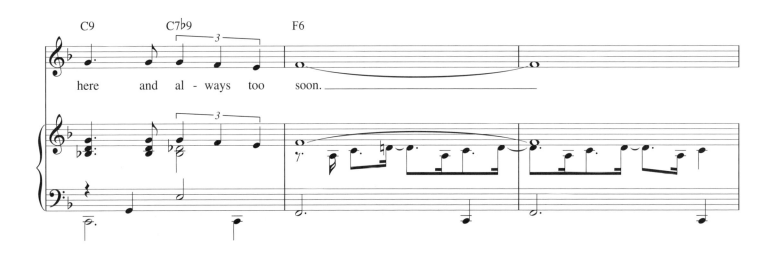

here and al - ways too soon. _____

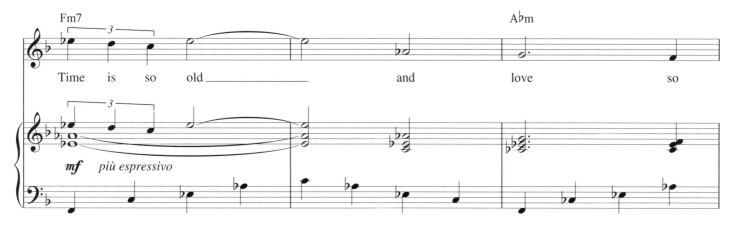

Time is so old _____ and love so

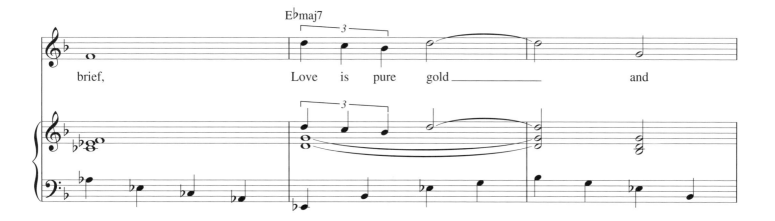

brief, Love is pure gold _____ and

time a thief. We're late, _____

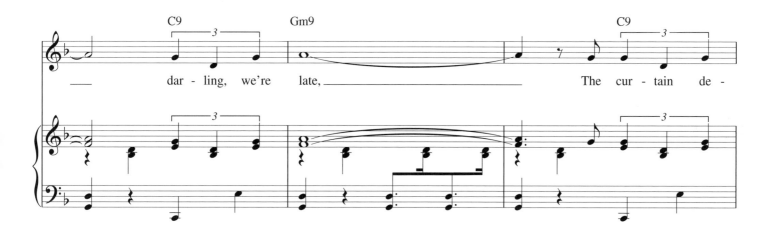

_____ dar - ling, we're late, _____ The cur - tain de -

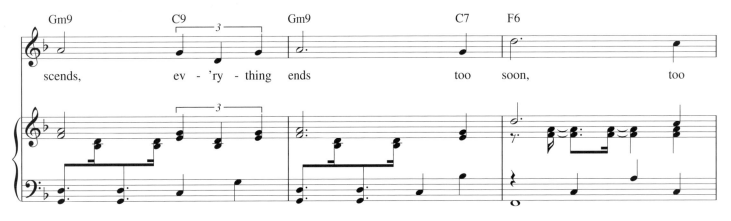

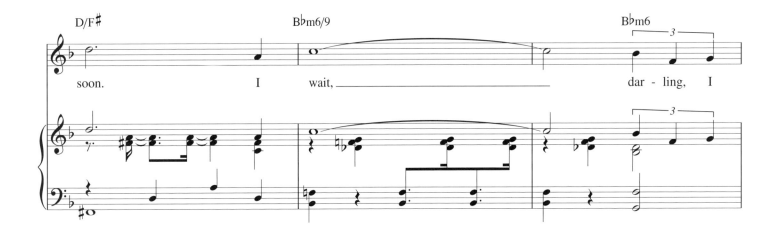

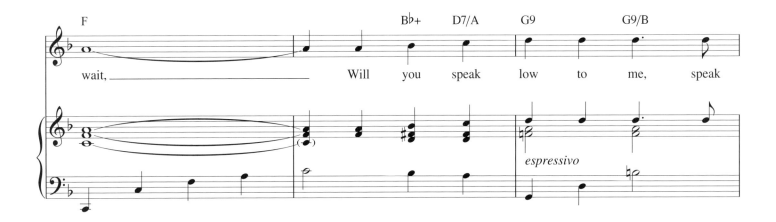

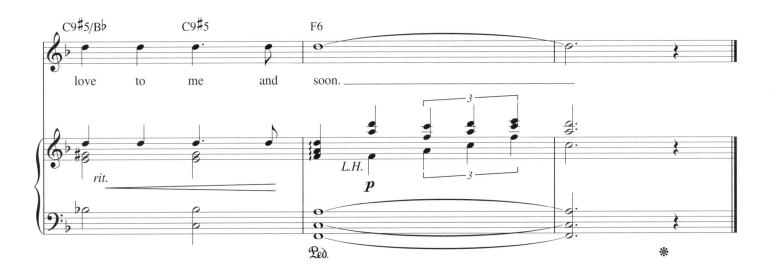

NOBODY MAKES A PASS AT ME

from *Pins and Needles*

Words and Music by
HAROLD ROME

I want men that I can squeeze, that I can please, that I can tease.

Two or three or four or more! What are those fools wait-ing for?

I want love and I want kiss-ing __ I want more of what I'm miss-ing. __

No-bod-y comes knock-ing at my front door. What do they think my knock-er's for? If they

don't come soon there won't be an-y more! What can the mat-ter be? I

Slow swing

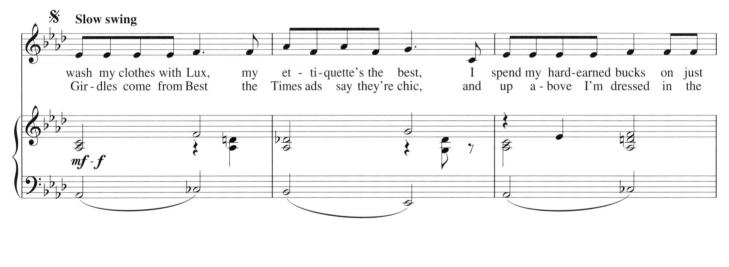

wash my clothes with Lux, my et-ti-quette's the best, I spend my hard-earned bucks on just
Gir-dles come from Best the Times ads say they're chic, and up a-bove I'm dressed in the

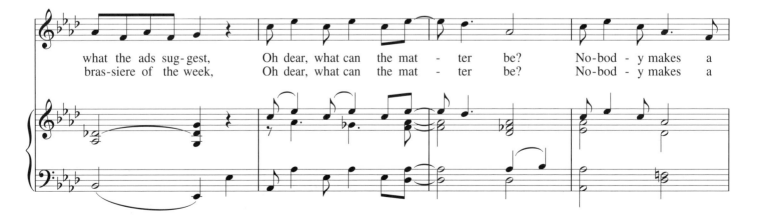

what the ads sug-gest, Oh dear, what can the mat-ter be? No-bod-y makes a
bras-siere of the week, Oh dear, what can the mat-ter be? No-bod-y makes a

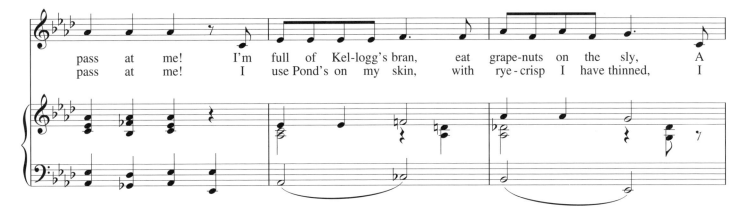

pass   at   me!   I'm   full   of   Kel-logg's bran,   eat   grape-nuts   on   the   sly,   A
pass   at   me!   I   use Pond's on   my   skin,   with   rye-crisp   I   have thinned,   I

date   is   on   the   can   of   the   cof-fee   that   I   buy.   Oh   dear,   what   can   the   mat-
get   my   cul-ture   in,   I   be-gan"Gone   with   the   Wind."   Oh   dear,   what   can   the   mat-

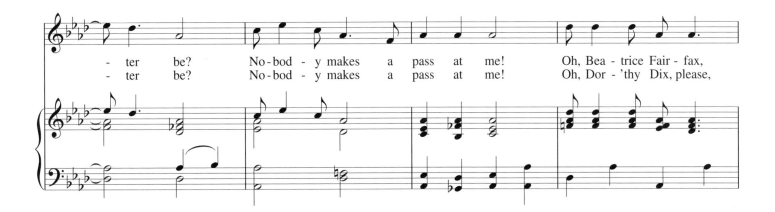

-ter   be?   No-bod-y   makes   a   pass   at   me!   Oh,   Bea-trice   Fair-fax,
-ter   be?   No-bod-y   makes   a   pass   at   me!   Oh,   Dor-'thy   Dix, please,

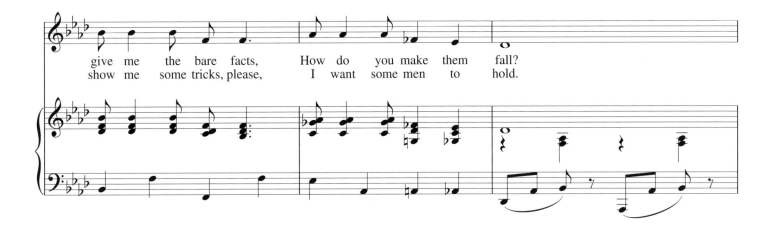

give   me   the   bare   facts,   How   do   you   make   them   fall?
show   me   some tricks, please,   I   want   some   men   to   hold.

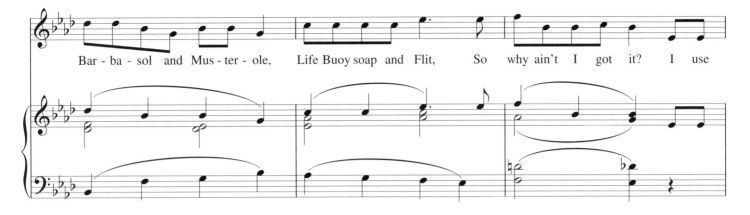

Bar-ba-sol and Mus-ter-ole, Life Buoy soap and Flit, So why ain't I got it? I use

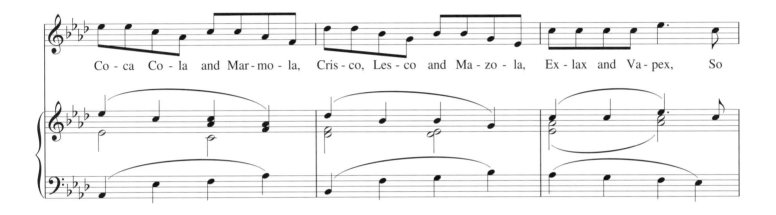

Co-ca Co-la and Mar-mo-la, Cris-co, Les-co and Ma-zo-la, Ex-lax and Va-pex, So

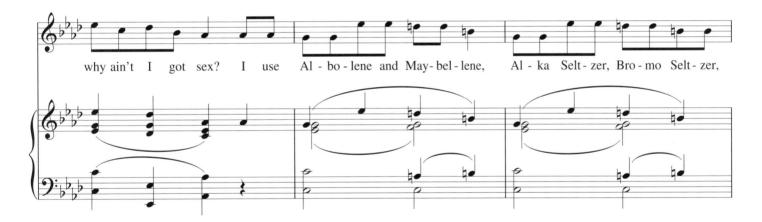

why ain't I got sex? I use Al-bo-lene and May-bel-lene, Al-ka Selt-zer, Bro-mo Selt-zer,

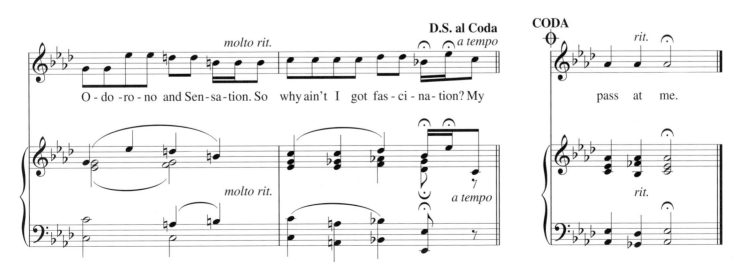

O-do-ro-no and Sen-sa-tion. So why ain't I got fas-ci-na-tion? My

pass at me.

BEWITCHED
from *Pal Joey*

Words by LORENZ HART
Music by RICHARD RODGERS

Moderately - In 2

VERA:

He's a fool and don't I know it.

But a fool can have his charms. I'm in love and don't I show it,

Like a babe in arms. Love's the same old sad sen - sa - tion.

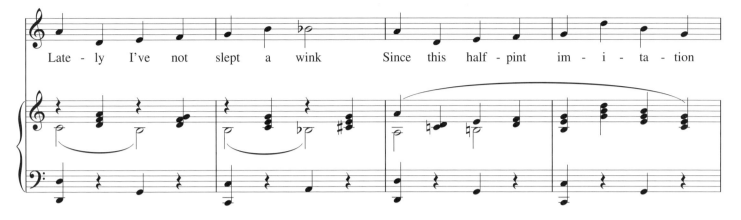

Late - ly I've not slept a wink Since this half - pint im - i - ta - tion

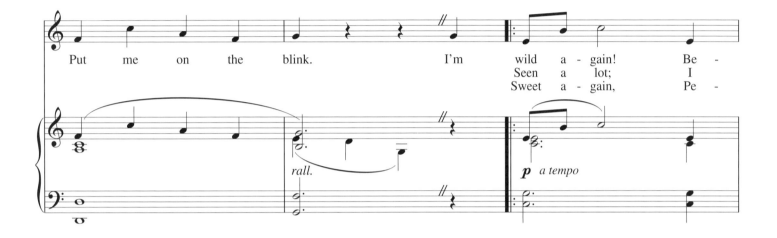

Put me on the blink. I'm
Seen a lot; I
Sweet a - gain, Pe -

wild a - gain! Be -
now

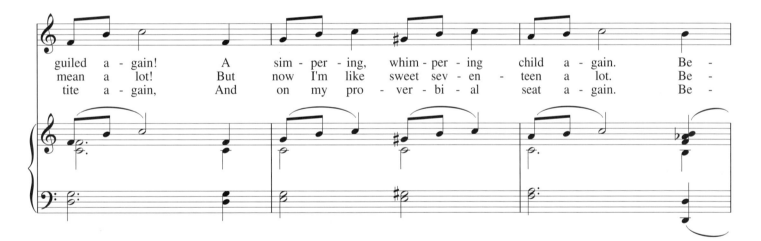

guiled a - gain! A sim - per - ing, whim - per - ing child a - gain. Be -
mean a lot! But now I'm like sweet sev - en - teen a lot. Be -
tite a - gain, And on my pro - ver - bi - al seat a - gain. Be -

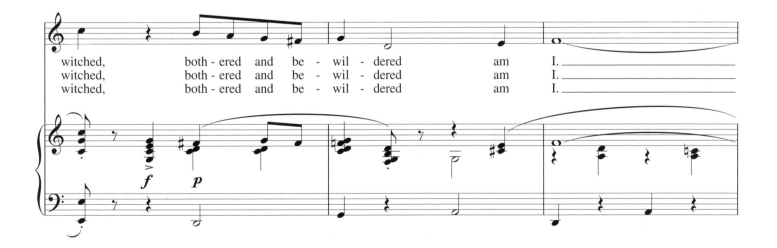

witched, both - ered and be - wil - dered am I.
witched, both - ered and be - wil - dered am I.
witched, both - ered and be - wil - dered am I.

He's a laugh, but I love it ____ Be-cause the laugh's on me. A
Hor - i - zon - tal - ly speak - ing, ____ He's at his ver - y best.
You might say we are clos - er ____ Than Roe - buck is to Sears. I'm

pill he is, But still he is All wine and I'll keep him un -
Vexed a - gain, Per - plexed a - gain, Thank God I can be o - ver -
dumb a - gain, And numb a - gain, A rich, read - y, ripe lit - tle

til he is Be - witched, both - ered and be - wil - dered like
sexed a - gain. Be - witched, both - ered and be - wil - dered am
plum a - gain. Be - witched, both - ered and be - wil - dered am

1, 2
me. _____
I. _____

3
I. _____

HOME
from *Phantom*

Words and Music by
MAURY YESTON

This song is a duet for the Phantom and Christine in the show, adapted as a solo for this edition.

Fa - ther said I would know __ the place, __ skin would tin - gle and pulse __

__ would race as they do, __ it's here! I'm

rit.

Faster ♩ = 112

home, where mu - sic fills the air, and I'm
Here, where fa - bles come a - live, year by

a tempo - più mosso

home, where a thou - sand lov - ers cry, swoon and sigh, and I'm
year we for - get our trou - bled nights un - der lights, and each

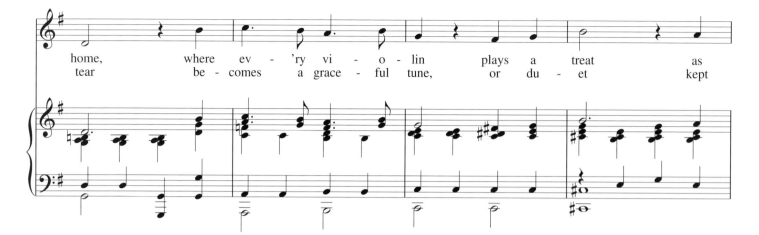

home, where ev - 'ry vi - o - lin plays a treat as
tear be - comes a grace - ful tune, or du - et kept

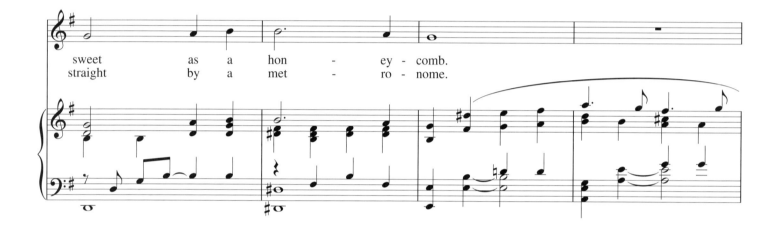

sweet as a hon - ey - comb.
straight by a met - ro - nome.

Wher - ev - er mu - sic plays, I know
And if I'm sing - ing then I know

I'm__ home.
I'm__

home.

Where ev - 'ry En - glish horn makes me feel

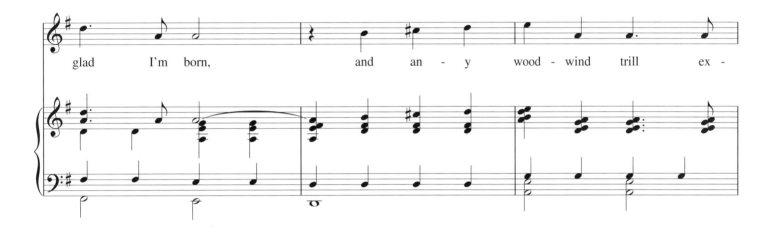

glad I'm born, and an - y wood - wind trill ex -

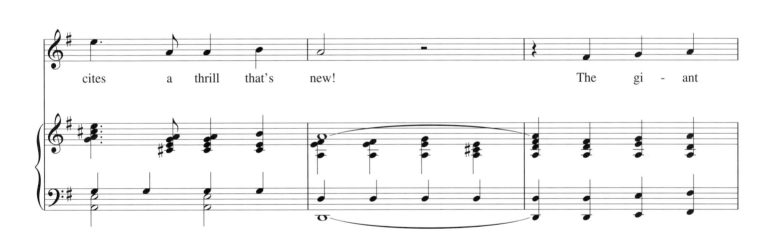

cites a thrill that's new! The gi - ant

con - tra - bass, the great so - pra - no's face,

com - bine to make a per - fect world far bet - ter than what's

out - side. Dreams, I've lived with - in my dreams,

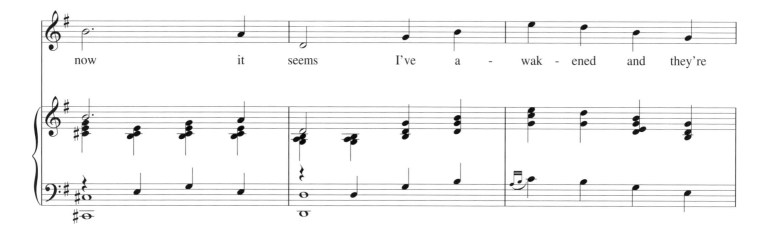

now it seems I've a - wak - ened and they're

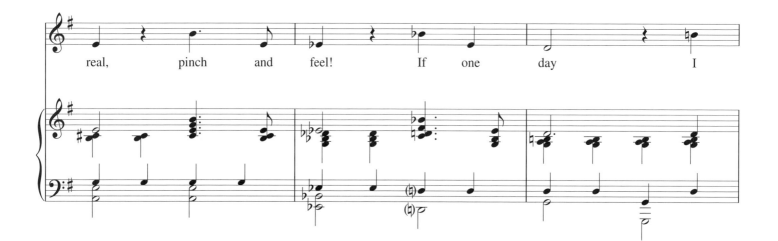

real, pinch and feel! If one day I

walk up-on this stage, from these wings, and play un-der-

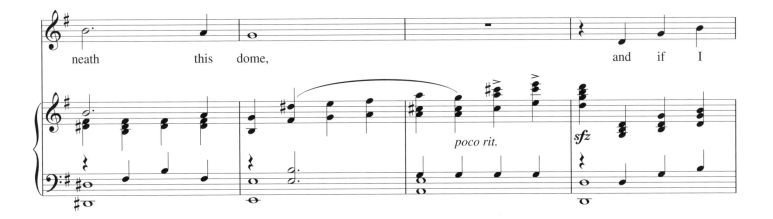

neath this dome, and if I

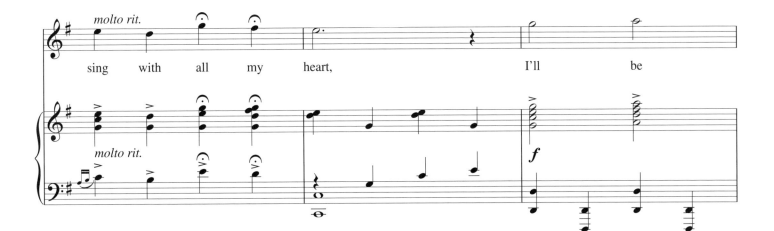

molto rit.

sing with all my heart, I'll be

home.

I'll SHOW HIM

from *Plain and Fancy*

Words by ARNOLD B. HORWITT
Music by ALBERT HAGUE

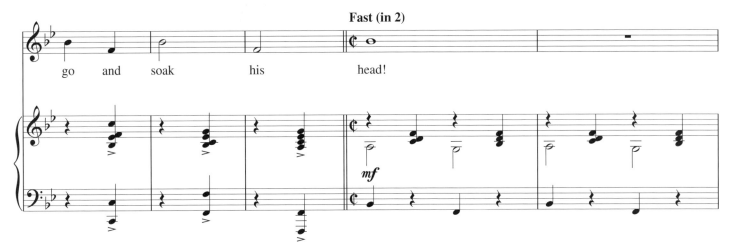

go and soak his head!

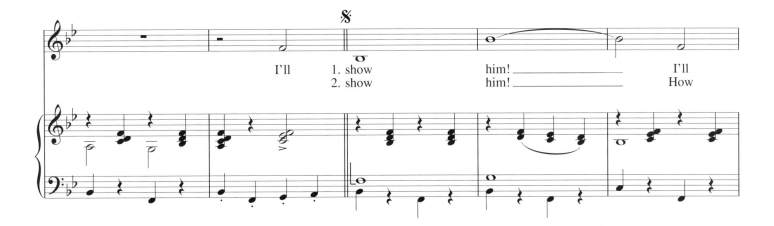

I'll 1. show him! _____ I'll
    2. show him! _____ How

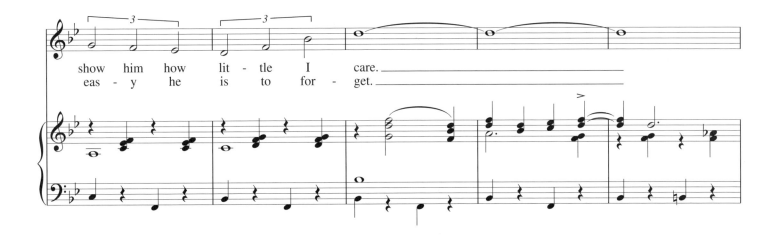

show him how lit - tle I care. _____
eas - y he is to for - get. _____

When we meet I'll just stand with my nose in the air! _____
In a week I won't e - ven re - mem - ber him, yet _____

Though he's sigh - ing,_____
I'll be flirt - ing,_____

And plead - ing and down on his knees _____
With fel - lers I don't e - ven know _____

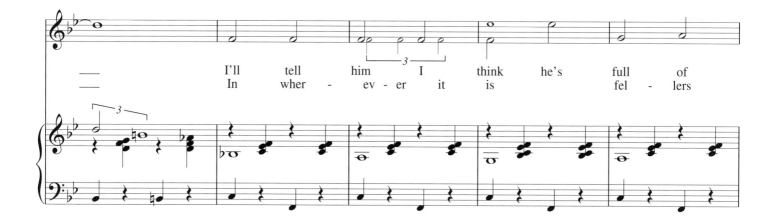

I'll tell him I think he's full of
In wher - ev - er it is fel - lers

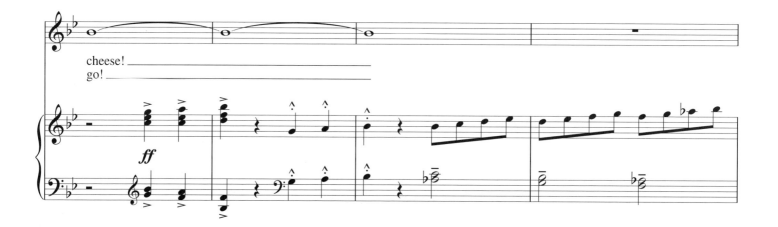

cheese! _____
go! _____

ff

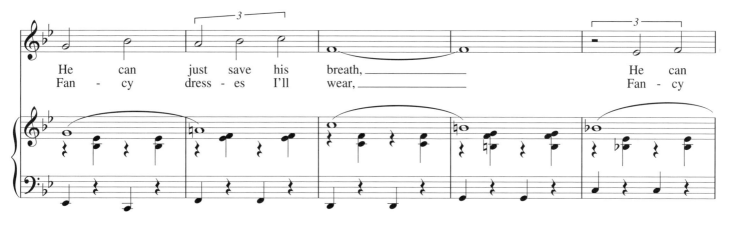

He can just save his breath, _____ He can
Fan - cy dress - es I'll wear, _____ Fan - cy

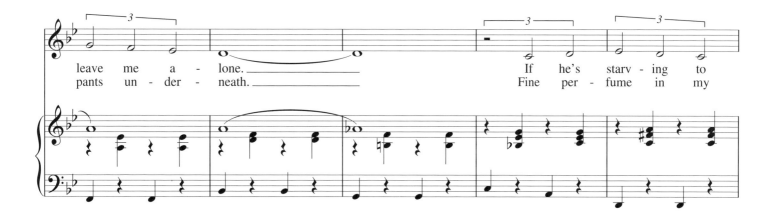

leave me a - lone. _____ If he's starv - ing to
pants un - der - neath. _____ Fine per - fume in my

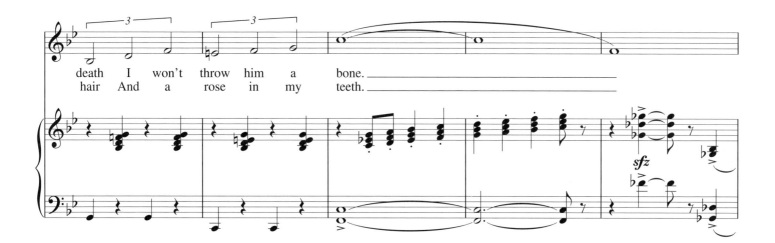

death I won't throw him a bone. _____
hair And a rose in my teeth. _____

sfz

I'll show him! How hap - py I am to be
I'll show him! I'll show him the way he showed

p

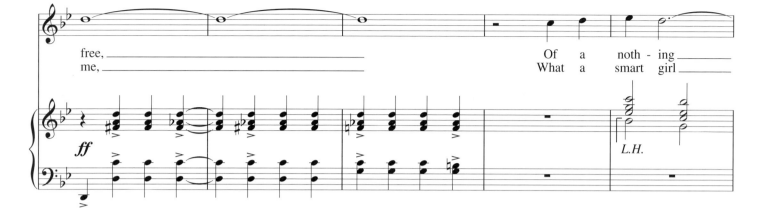

Of a noth-ing ___ / What a smart girl ___
free, ___ / me, ___

To Coda ⊕   **Tempo I**

___ who's noth-ing to me. ___
___ a lum - mox

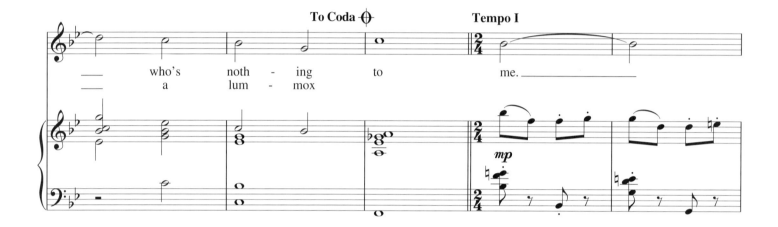

He'll find out I'm not yet such a ba - by, ___

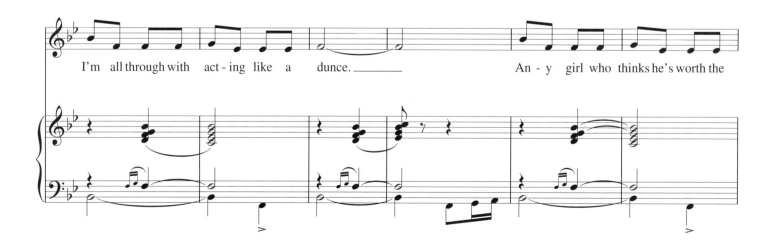

I'm all through with act-ing like a dunce. ___ An - y girl who thinks he's worth the

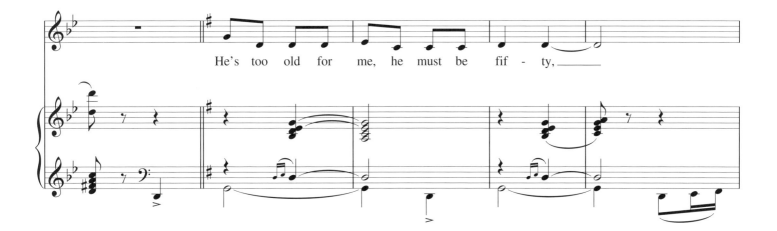

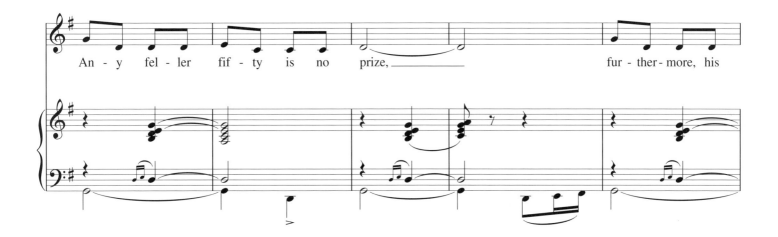

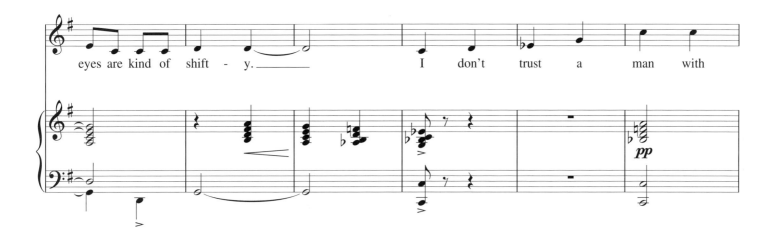

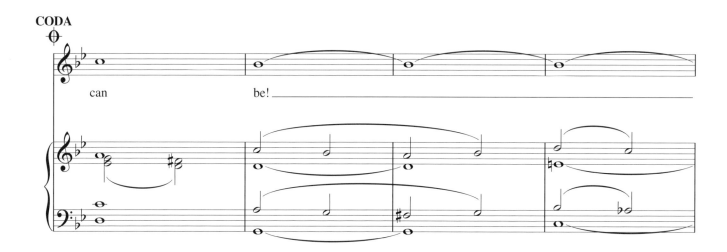

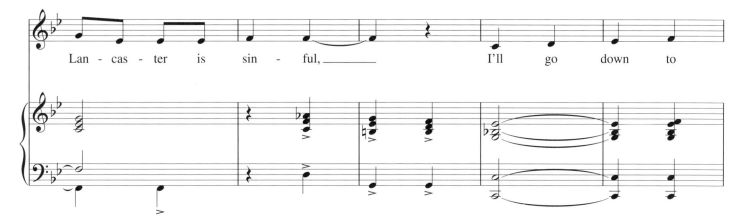

Lan - cas - ter is sin - ful, _____ I'll go down to

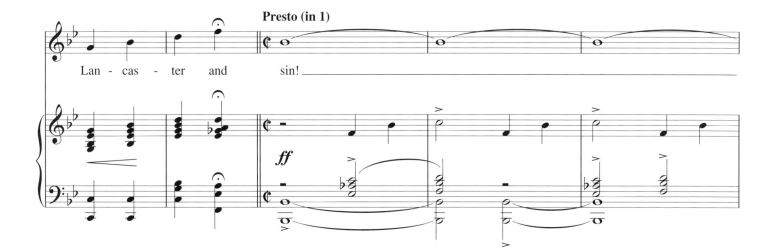

Presto (in 1)

Lan - cas - ter and sin! _____

ff

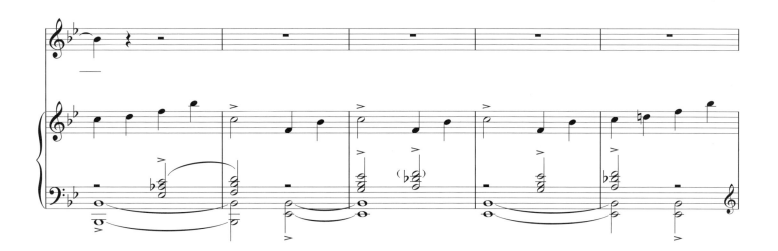

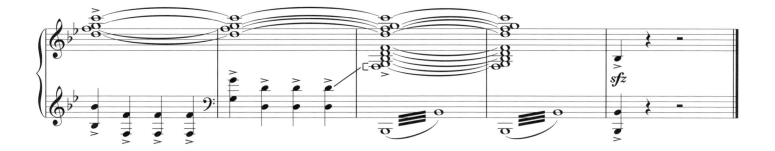

sfz

CHILDREN OF THE WIND

from *Rags*

Lyric by STEPHEN SCHWARTZ
Music by CHARLES STROUSE

Da - vid, did __ they hurt you, dar - ling? Show me where __ they hurt you, dar - ling.

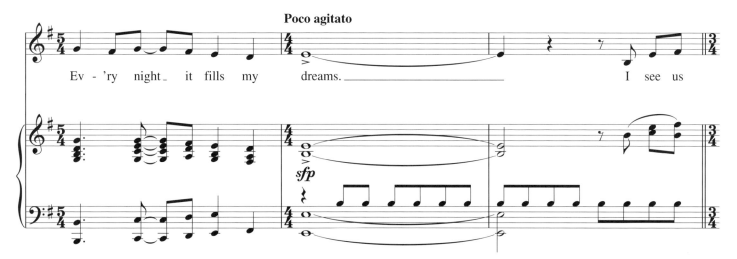

Poco agitato

Ev - 'ry night __ it fills my dreams. _____ I see us

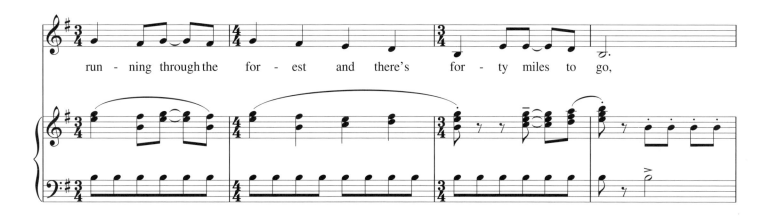

run - ning through the for - est and there's for - ty miles to go,

sneak - ing past __ the bor - der in the si - lent snow,

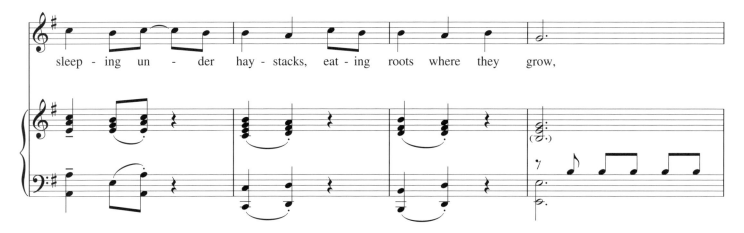

sleep - ing un - der hay - stacks, eat - ing roots where they grow,

beg - ging on __ the pier at Dan - zig. Well, we made __ it here from Dan - zig;

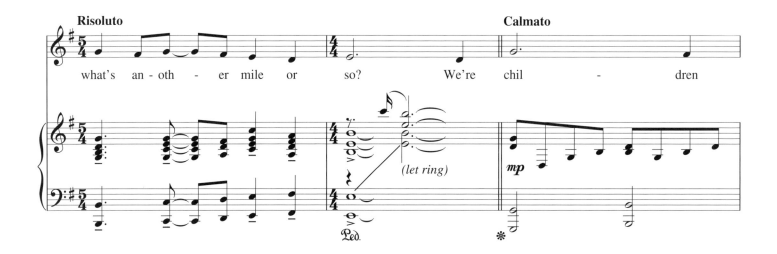

Risoluto   **Calmato**

what's an - oth - er mile or so? We're chil - dren

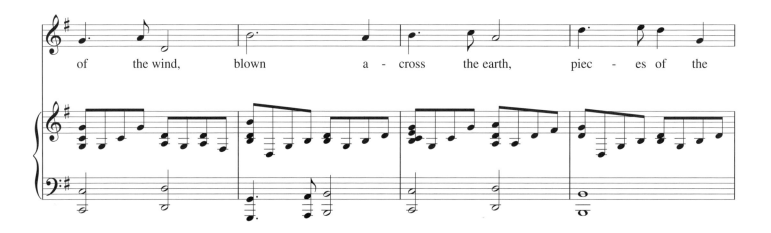

of the wind, blown a - cross the earth, piec - es of the

heart   scat - tered worlds a - part,   so far   from

those   we love,   all   the   chil - dren of   the wind.

There's a morn-ing I want some-day to see;   all the chil-dren of my

chil - dren are there.   And they're ver - y, ver - y nois - y,   run-ning through my

kitch - en.   And we've been there   for a life - time.   And I'll know then

they will nev - er   be _____

chil - dren   of   the wind,   long - ing   to   be   one

half   a world a - way.   We   will make   our

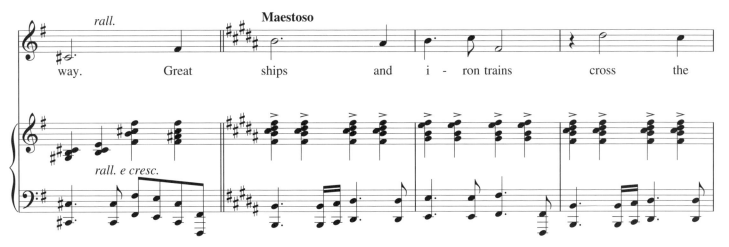

way. Great ships and i - ron trains cross the

seas and plains, take us to the day.

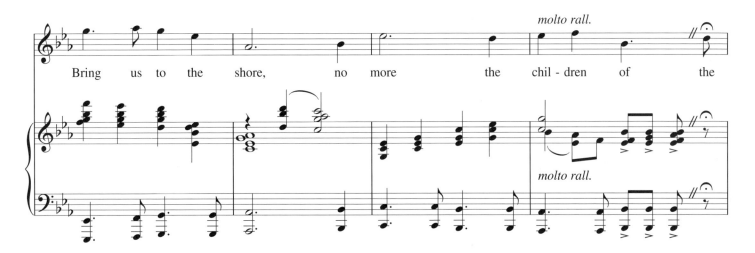

Bring us to the shore, no more the chil - dren of the

wind.

YOUR DADDY'S SON

from *Ragtime*

Words and Music by STEPHEN FLAHERTY
and LYNN AHRENS

Moderately slow

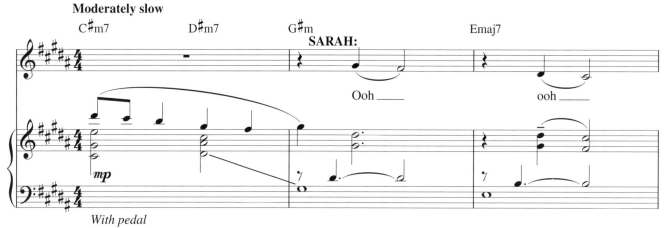

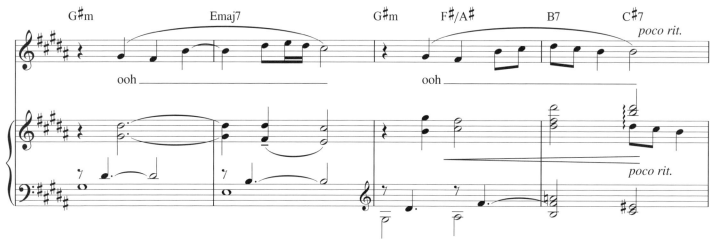

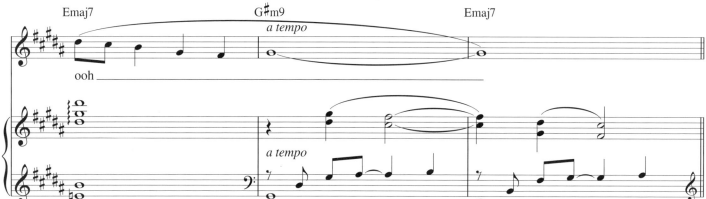

catch you like a spell. He could make you love him 'fore the tune was done.

You have your Dad-dy's hands. You are your Dad-dy's son.

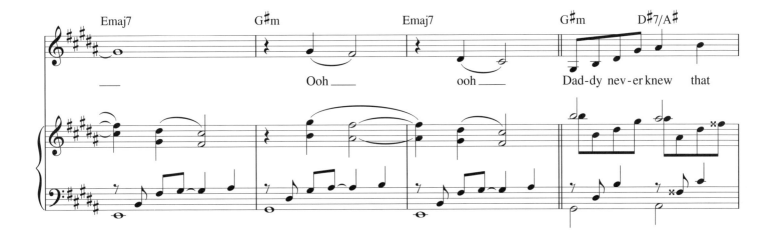

Ooh ___ ooh ___ Dad-dy nev-er knew that

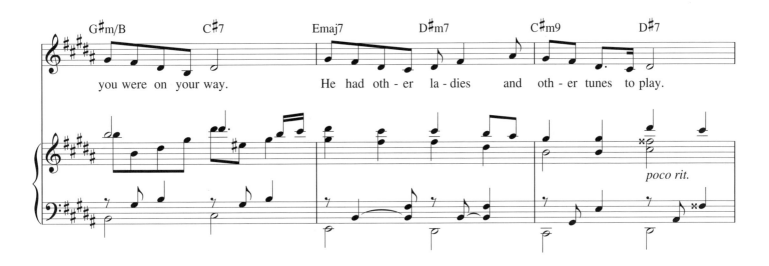

you were on your way. He had oth-er la-dies and oth-er tunes to play.

HE PLAYS THE VIOLIN

from *1776*

Words and Music by
SHERMAN EDWARDS

Brightly

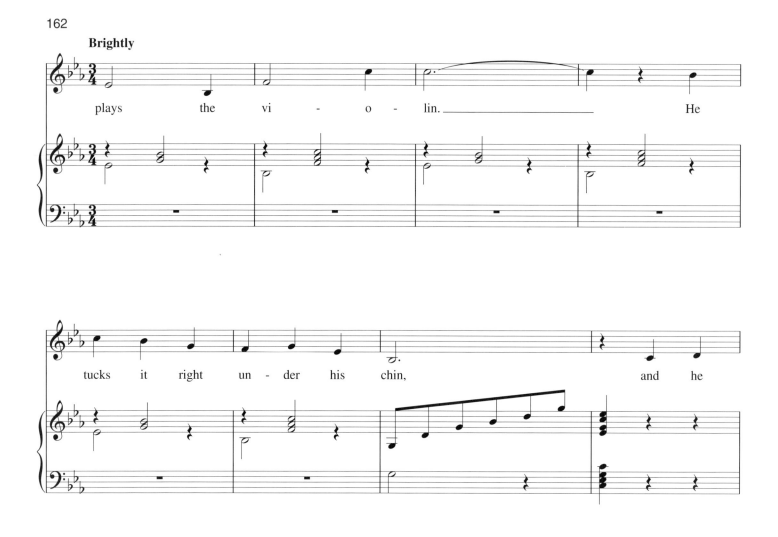

plays the vi - o - lin. _____ He

tucks it right un - der his chin, and he

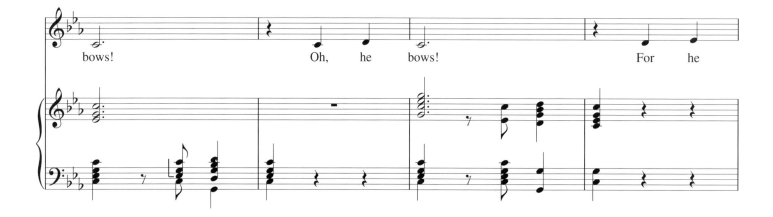

bows! Oh, he bows! For he

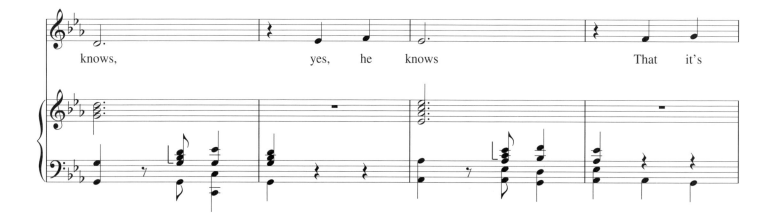

knows, yes, he knows That it's

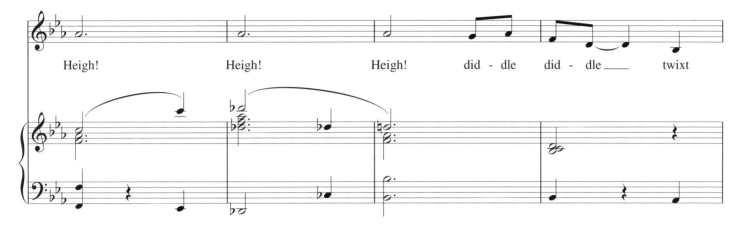

Heigh!   Heigh!   Heigh!   did - dle   did - dle ____ twixt

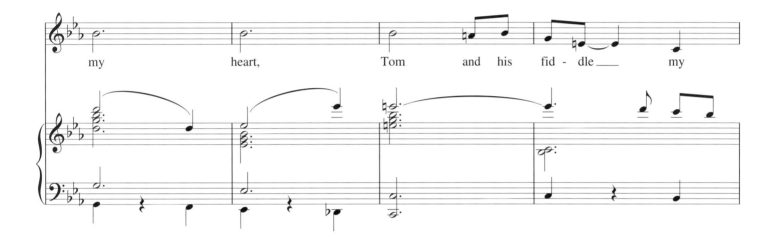

my   heart,   Tom   and   his   fid - dle ____ my

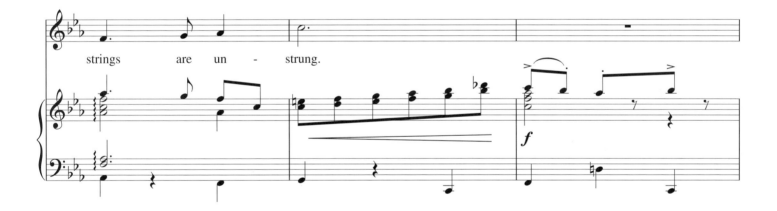

strings   are   un - strung.

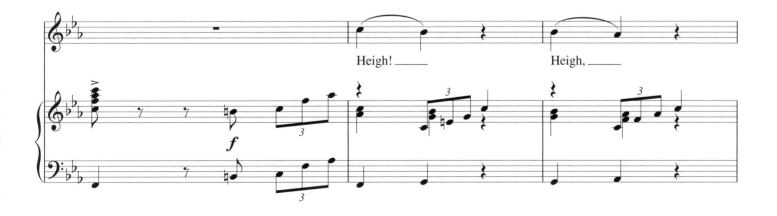

Heigh! ____   Heigh, ____

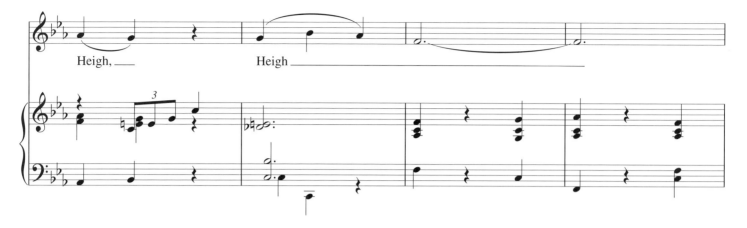

Heigh, ___ Heigh ___

I ___ am un - done. ___

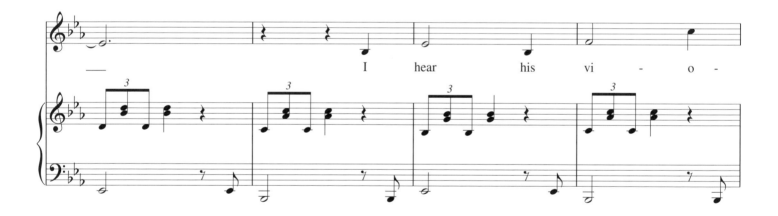

I hear his vi - o -

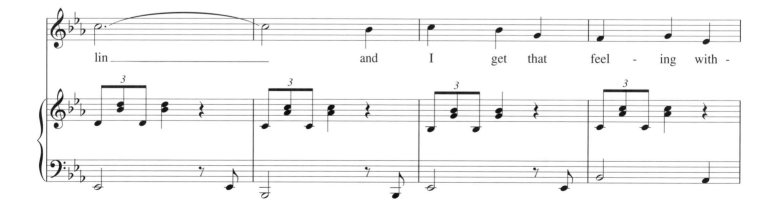

lin ___ and I get that feel - ing with -

in, _____ And I sigh! Oh, I

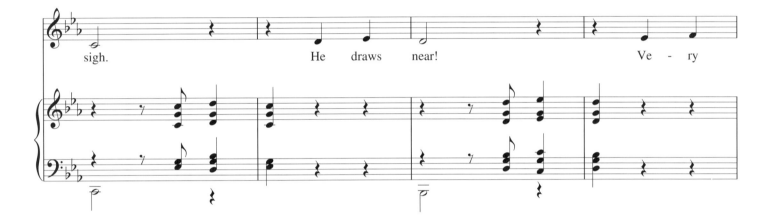

sigh. He draws near! Ve - ry

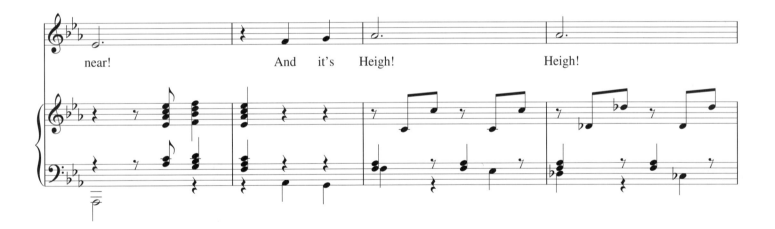

near! And it's Heigh! Heigh!

Heigh did - dle did - dle and "good

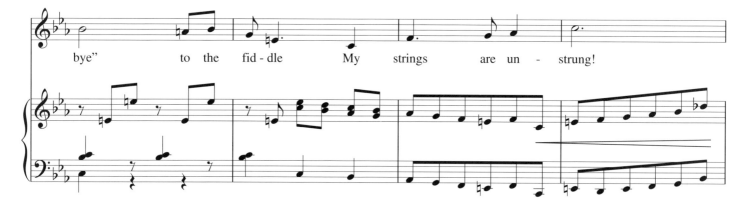

bye" to the fid - dle My strings are un - strung!

Heigh! Heigh,

Heigh, Heigh,

I am un - strung.

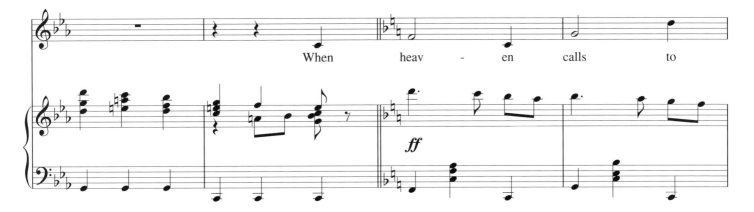

When heav - en calls to

me _____ sing me no sad el - e -

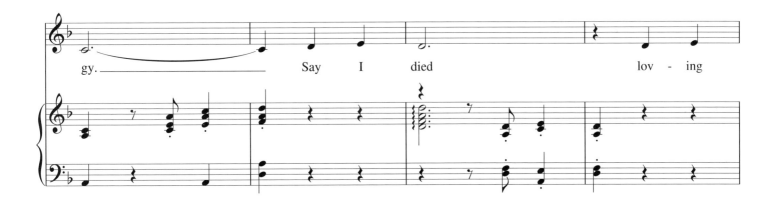

gy. _____ Say I died lov - ing

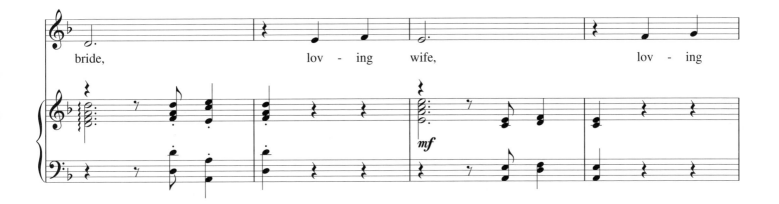

bride, lov - ing wife, lov - ing

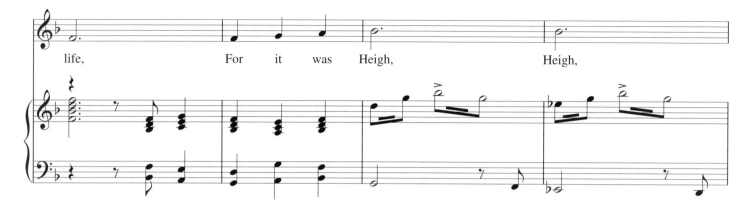

life, For it was Heigh, Heigh,

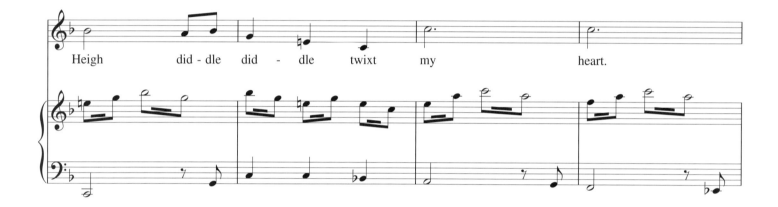

Heigh did - dle did - dle twixt my heart.

Tom and his fid - dle and ev - er will be.

Heigh, ___ heigh, ___

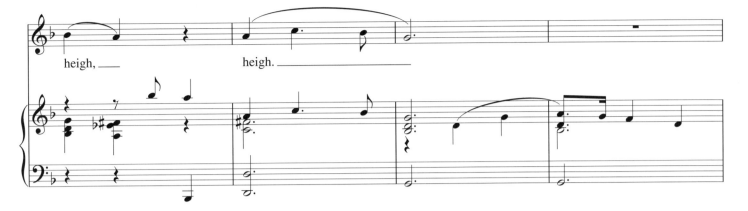

heigh, ___ heigh. ___

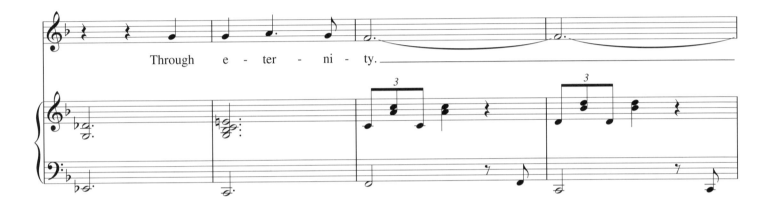

Through e - ter - ni - ty. ___

he plays the vi - o -

lin. ___

ff

YESTERDAYS
from *Roberta*

Words by OTTO HARBACH
Music by JEROME KERN

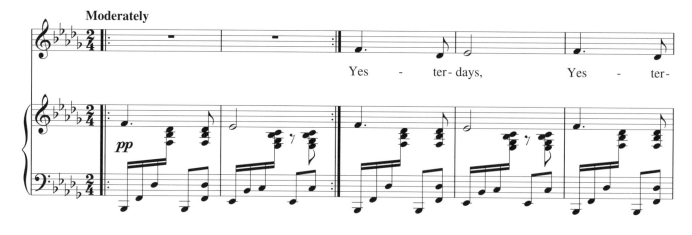

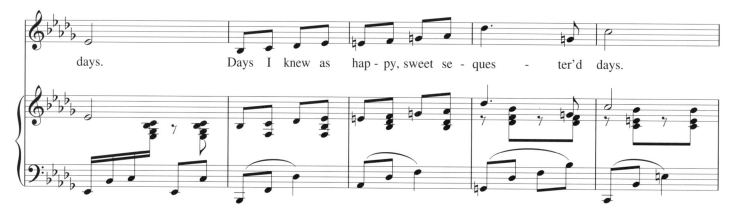

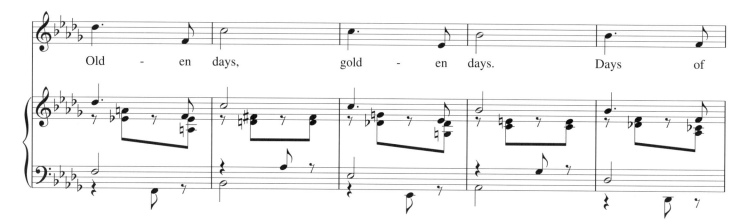

Truth was mine, Joy-ous, free and flam-ing life, for-sooth, was

mine. Sad am I, Glad am I, for to-

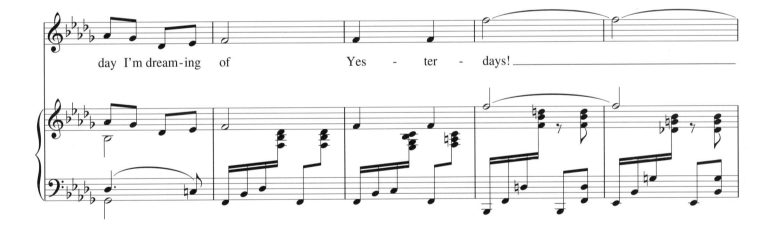

day I'm dream-ing of Yes - ter - days! _____

VANILLA ICE CREAM
from *She Loves Me*

Words by SHELDON HARNICK
Music by JERRY BOCK

AMALIA:

(Spoken:) Dear Friend: I am so sor-ry a-bout last night. It was a night-mare in ev-'ry way, But, to-geth-er, you and I will laugh at last night some day. Ice cream... he bought me ice cream... va-nil-la ice cream... I-mag-ine

Slow Polka

accel. poco a poco

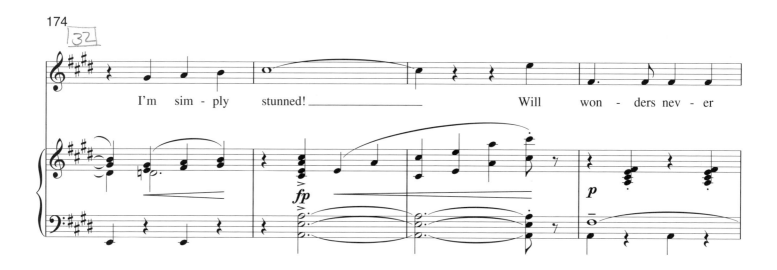

32

I'm sim - ply stunned! _____ Will won - ders nev - er

36

cease? Will won - ders nev - er cease? It's been a most pe -

40

cu - liar day! _____ Will won - ders nev - er

44

cease? Will won - der nev - er cease? *(Spoken:) Oh!*
Where was I?

59

63

67

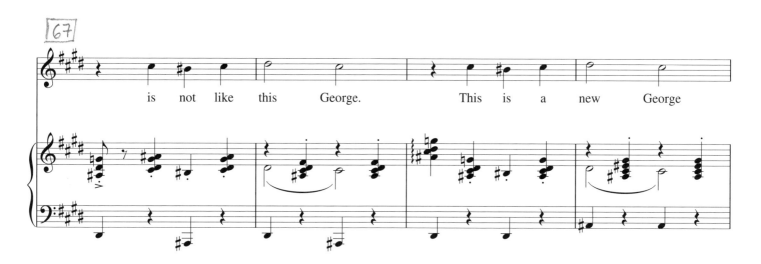

71

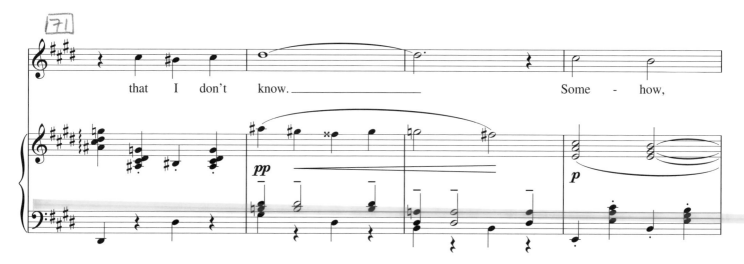

it all re-minds me of Doc-tor Jek - yll

and Mis - ter Hyde._____ For right be-fore my

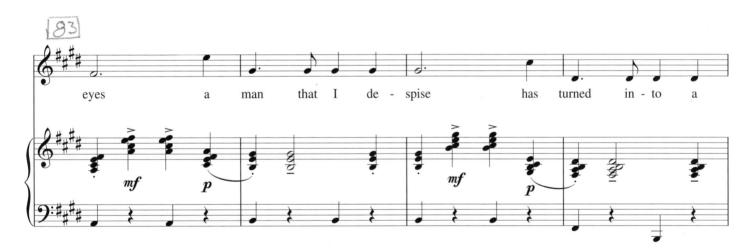

eyes a man that I de - spise has turned in - to a

man I like! It's al - most like a

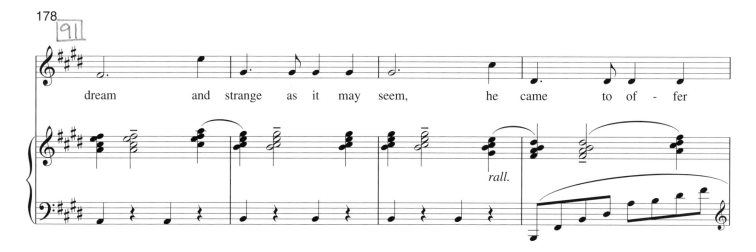

dream and strange as it may seem, he came to of -fer

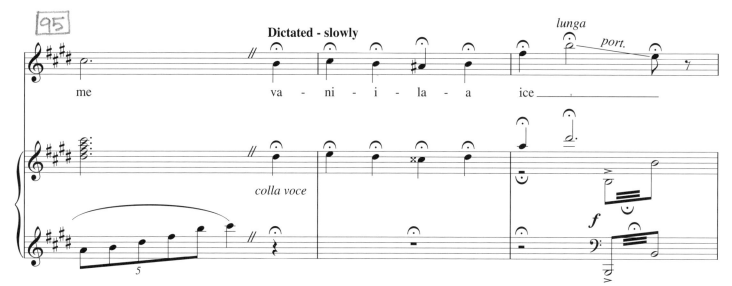

me va - ni - i - la - a ice

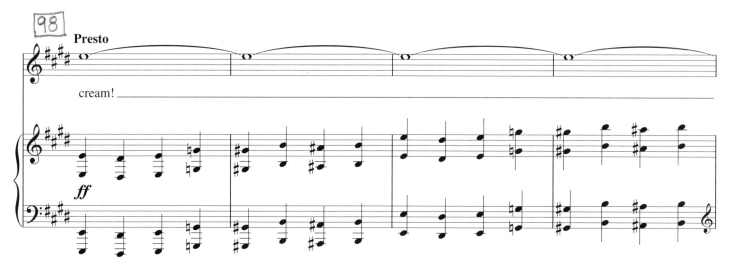

cream!

MAKE BELIEVE
from *Show Boat*

Lyrics by OSCAR HAMMERSTEIN II
Music by JEROME KERN

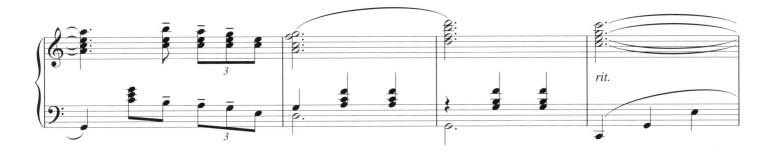

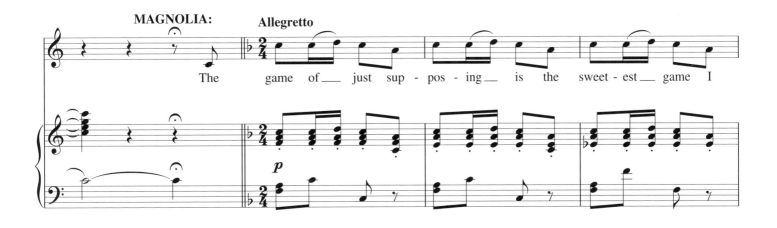

This song is a duet for Magnolia and Ravenal in the show, adapted as a solo for this edition.

see. And if the things we dream a - bout don't hap - pen __ to be
so, ___ That's _ just an un - im - port - ant tech - ni - cal - i -
Poco animato (𝅗𝅥 = ♩)
ty. Tho' the cold and bru - tal fact is
You and I have nev - er met, We need not

mind con - ven - tion's P's and Q's.

If we put our thoughts in prac - tice We can ban - ish all re -

gret, I - mag - in - ing most an - y -

thing we choose. We could

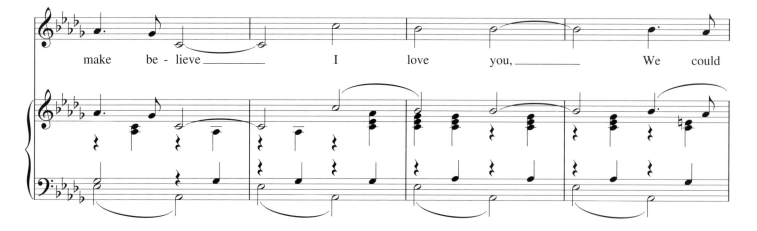

make be - lieve _____ I love you, _____ We could

make be - lieve _____ that you love me. _____ Oth - ers

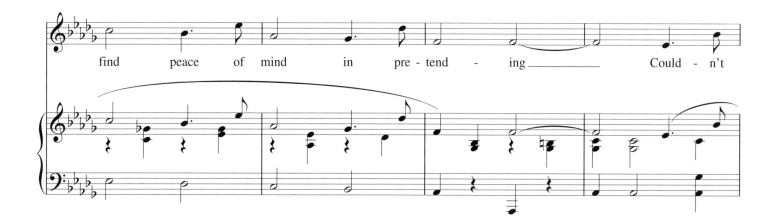

find peace of mind in pre - tend - ing _____ Could - n't

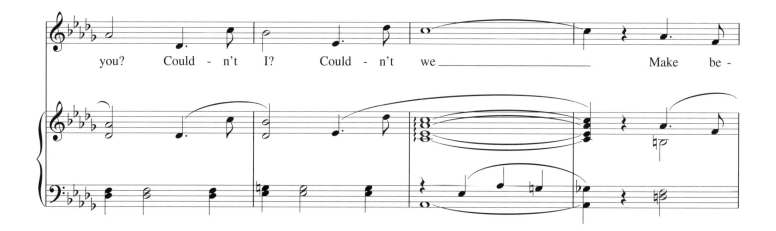

you? Could - n't I? Could - n't we _____ Make be -

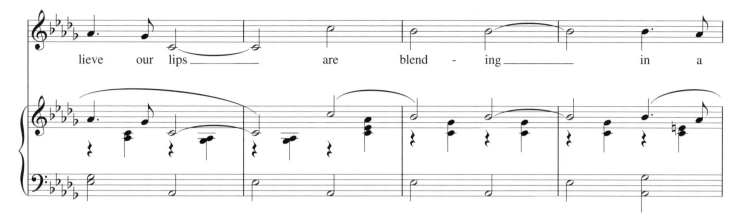

lieve our lips _____ are blend - ing _____ in a

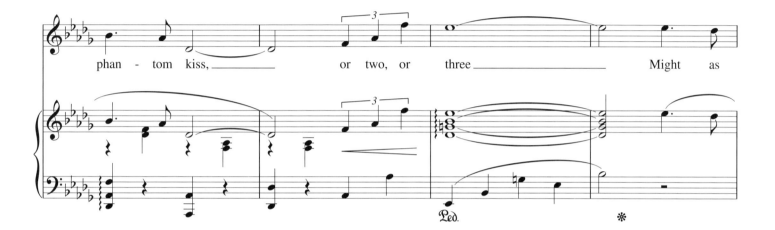

phan - tom kiss, _____ or two, or three _____ Might as

well make be - lieve I love you. _____ For, to

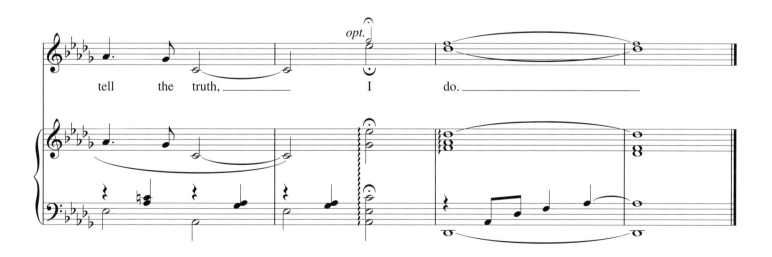

tell the truth, _____ I do. _____

WHY DO I LOVE YOU?

from *Show Boat*

Lyrics by OSCAR HAMMERSTEIN II
Music by JEROME KERN

This song is a duet for Magnolia and Ravenal in the show, adapted as a solo for this edition.

heav - en _____ (There's more than sev - en, _____ my heart dis -

cov - ers.) In this sweet im - prob - a - ble and un - real

world, Find - ing you has giv - en me my i - deal world.

Why do I love you? Why do you love me?

mp

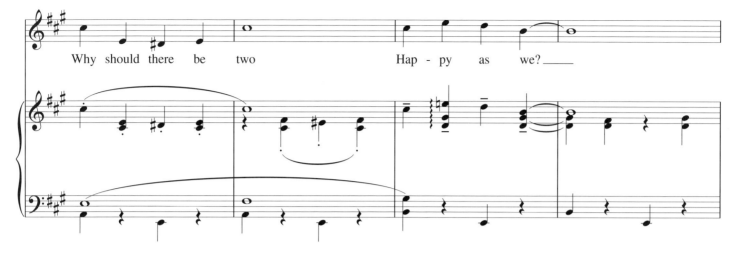

Why should there be two Hap - py as we?____

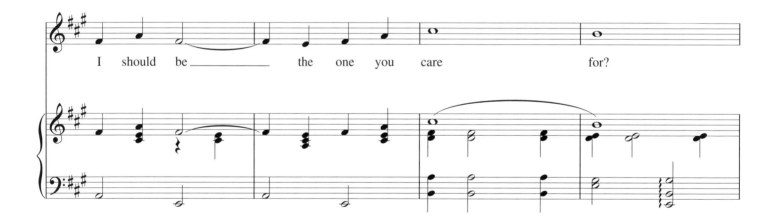

Can you see _____ the why or where - fore

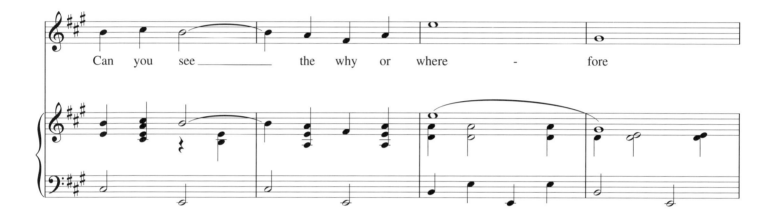

I should be _____ the one you care for?

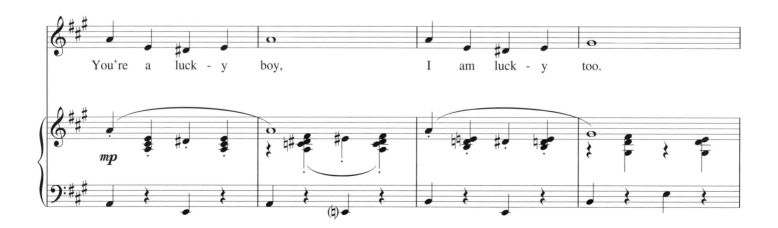

You're a luck - y boy, I am luck - y too.

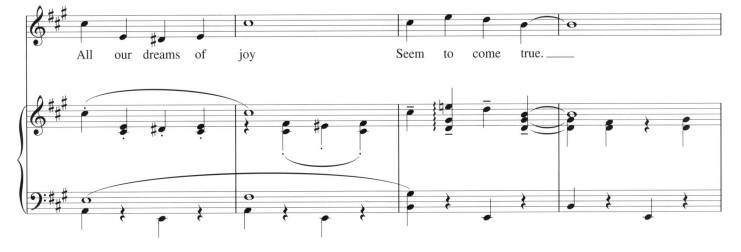

All our dreams of joy Seem to come true. ____

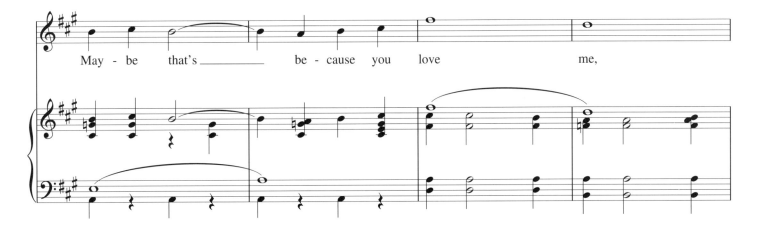

May - be that's ____ be - cause you love me,

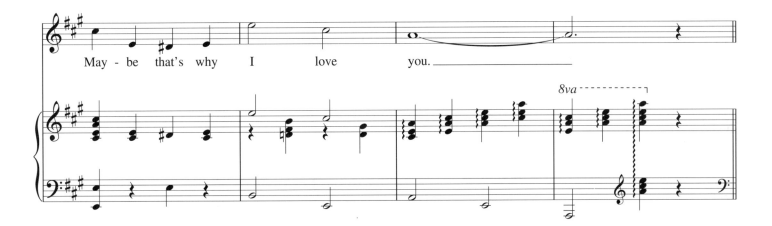

May - be that's why I love you. _____

8va

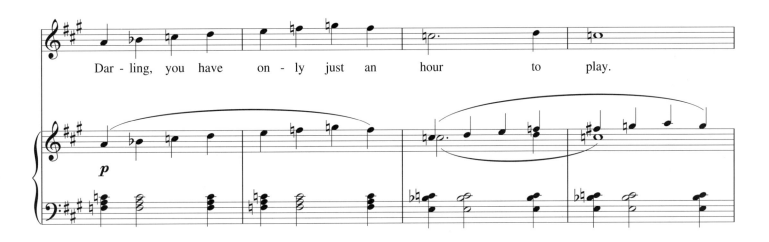

Dar - ling, you have on - ly just an hour to play.

p

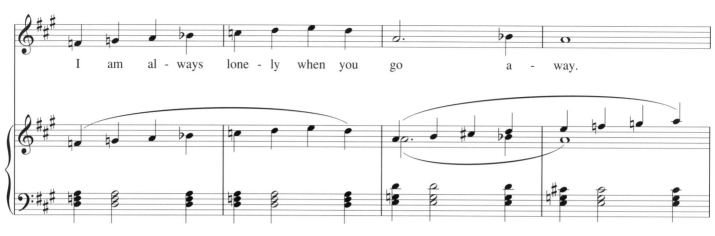

I am al - ways lone - ly when you go a - way.

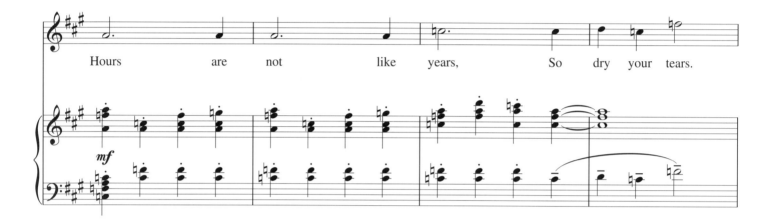

Hours are not like years, So dry your tears.

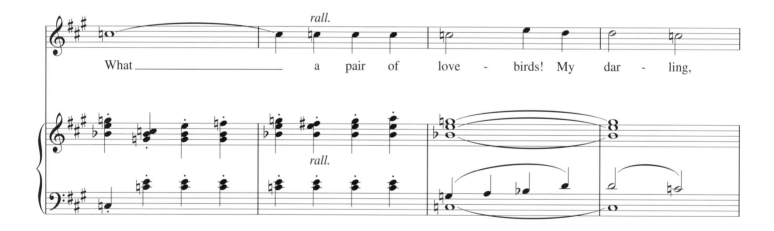

rall.

What _____ a pair of love - birds! My dar - ling,

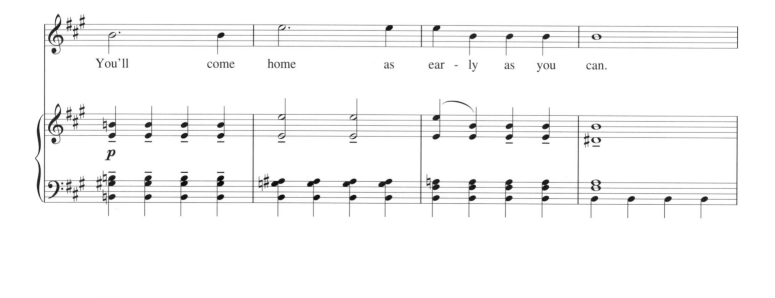

You'll come home as ear - ly as you can.

Mean - while I'll be good and pa - tient with my man.

Why do I love you? Why do you love me?

Why should there be two Hap - py as we? ____

Can you see ____ the why or where - fore?

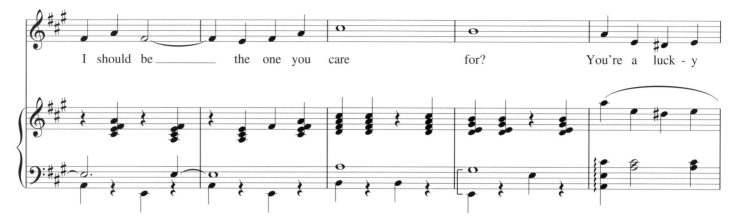

I should be _____ the one you care for? You're a luck-y

boy, I am luck-y too; All our dreams of joy

seem to come true. ____ May-be that's _____ be-cause you love

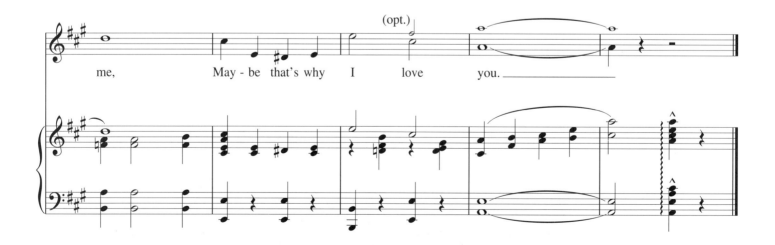

me, May-be that's why I love you. _____

HE WAS TOO GOOD TO ME

from *Simple Simon*

Words by LORENZ HART
Music by RICHARD RODGERS

193

I WONDER WHAT BECAME OF ME

from *St. Louis Woman*

Words by JOHNNY MERCER
Music by HAROLD ARLEN

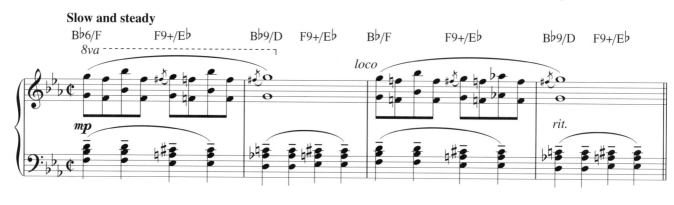

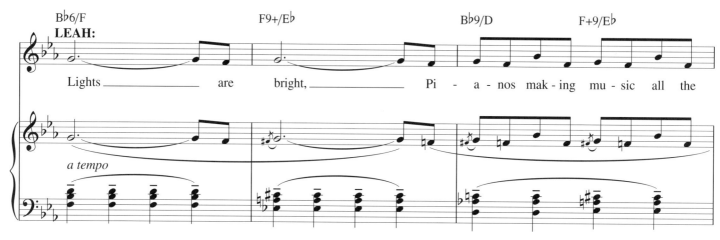

Lights ____ are bright, ____ Pi - a - nos mak - ing mu - sic all the

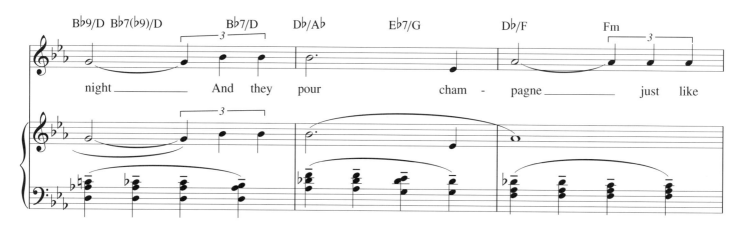

night ____ And they pour cham - pagne ____ just like

it was rain. ____ It's a sight to see, But I

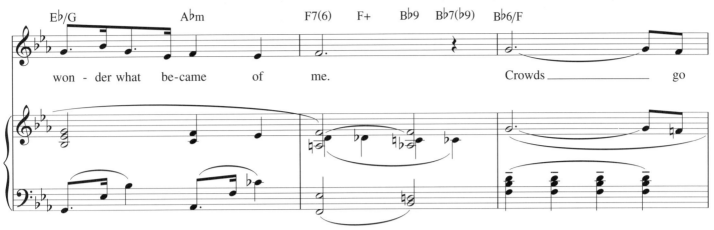

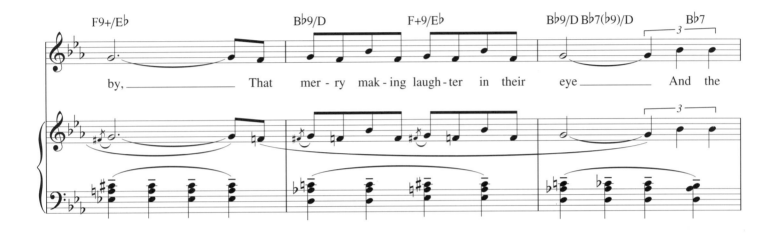

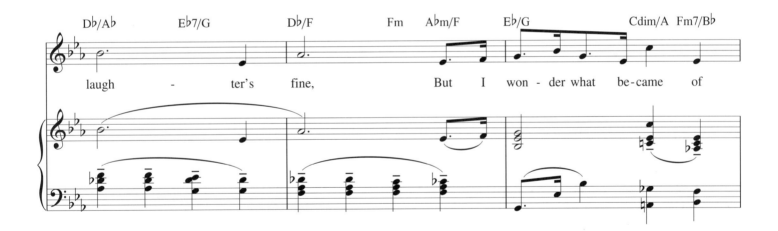

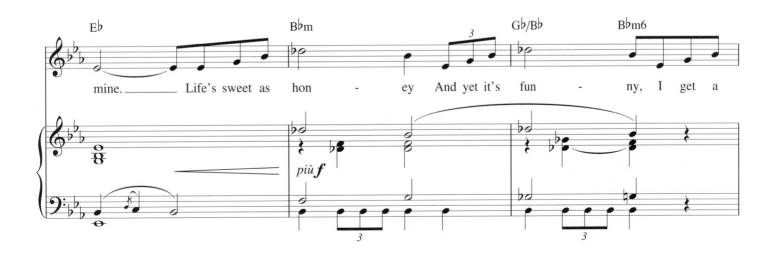

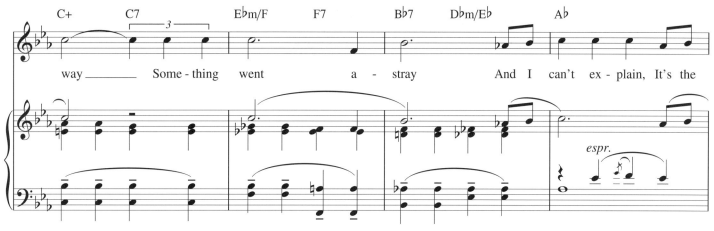

way _____ Some - thing went a - stray And I can't ex - plain, It's the

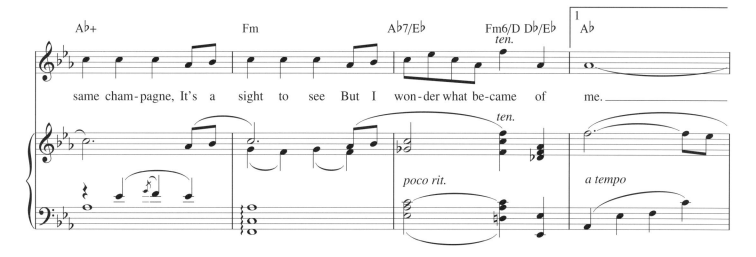

same cham - pagne, It's a sight to see But I won - der what be - came of me. _____

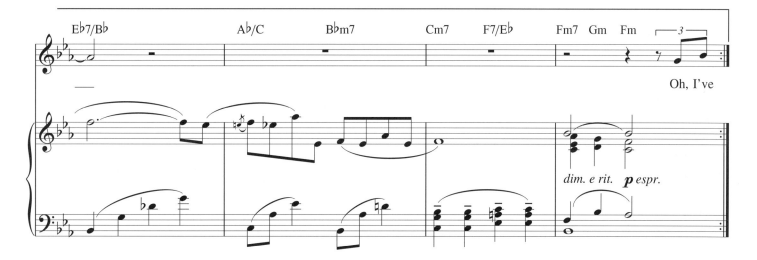

Oh, I've

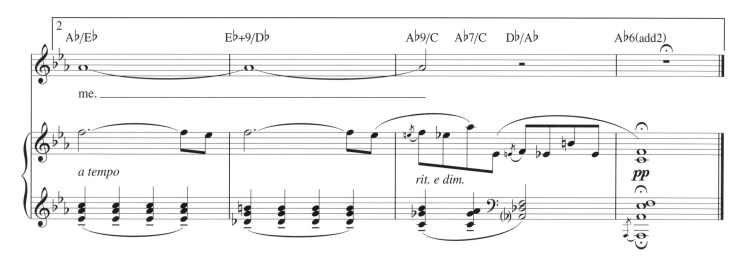

me. _____

FOLLOW YOUR HEART
from *Urinetown*

Music and Lyrics by MARK HOLLMANN
Book and Lyrics by GREG KOTIS

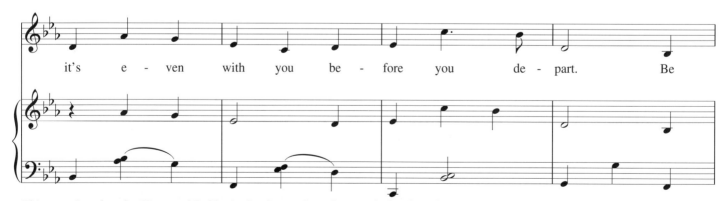

This song is a duet for Hope and Bobby in the show, adapted as a solo for this edition.

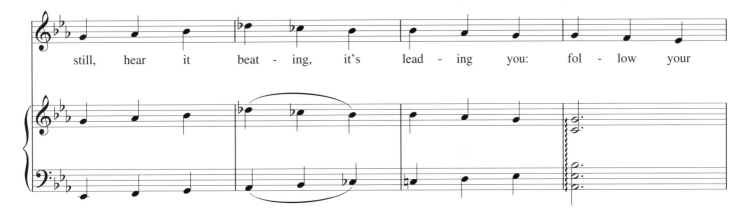

still, hear it beat - ing, it's lead - ing you: fol - low your

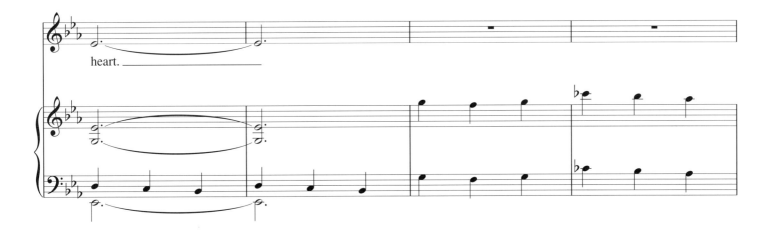

heart.

rit.   *a tempo*

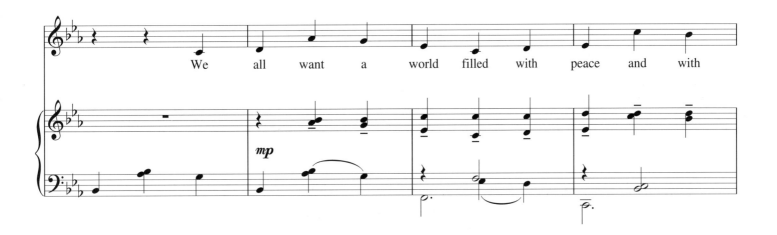

We all want a world filled with peace and with

mp

joy, with plen - ty of wa - ter for each girl and

boy. That bright, shin - ing world is just wait - ing to

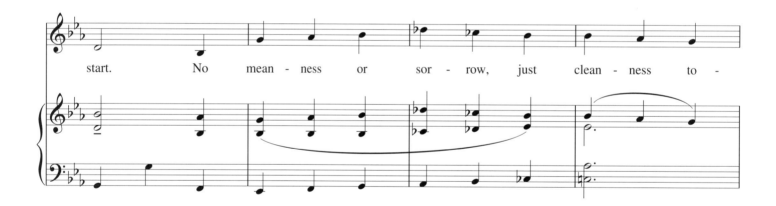

start. No mean - ness or sor - row, just clean - ness to -

mor - row, if on - ly you fol - low your heart. _____

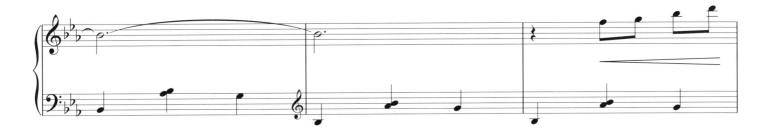

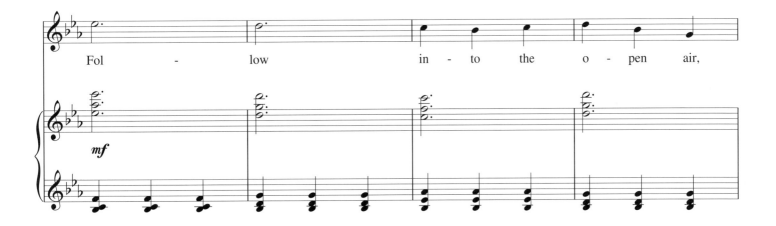

Fol - low in - to the o - pen air,

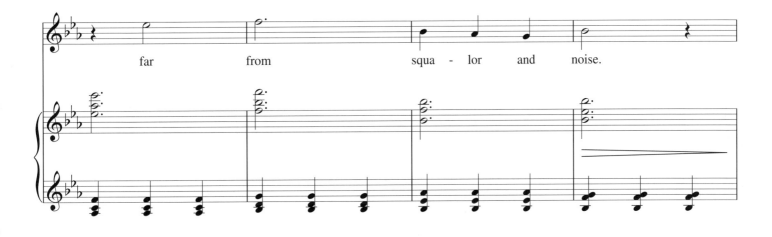

far from squa - lor and noise.

Fol - low, some - one is

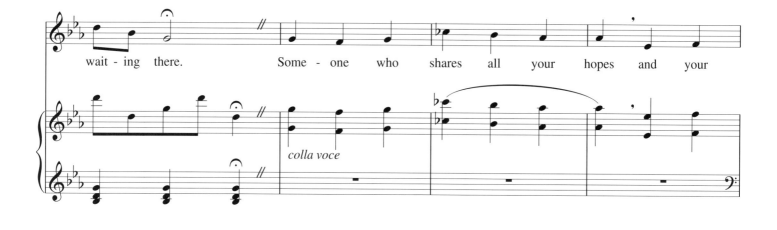

wait - ing there. Some - one who shares all your hopes and your

colla voce

joys. Some day I'll meet

a tempo

some - one whose heart joins with mine, a - or - tas and ar - ter - ies

all in - ter - twined. They'll beat so much strong - er than

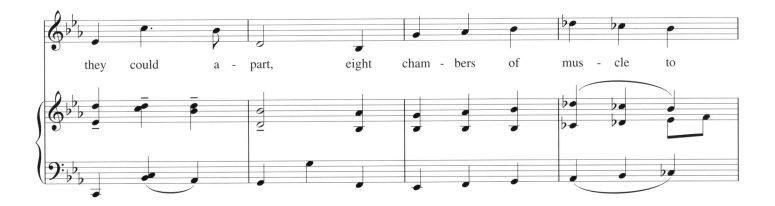

they could a - part, eight cham - bers of mus - cle to

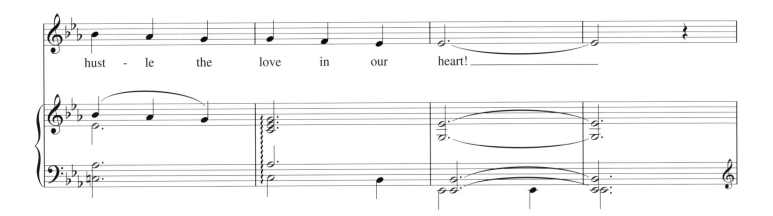

hust - le the love in our heart!

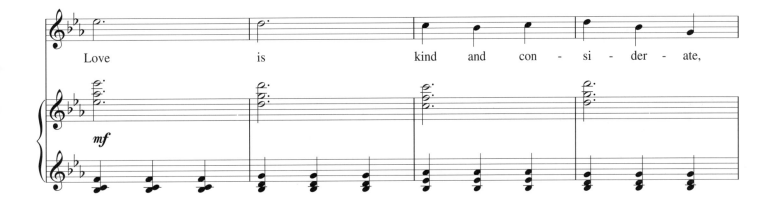

Love is kind and con - si - der - ate,

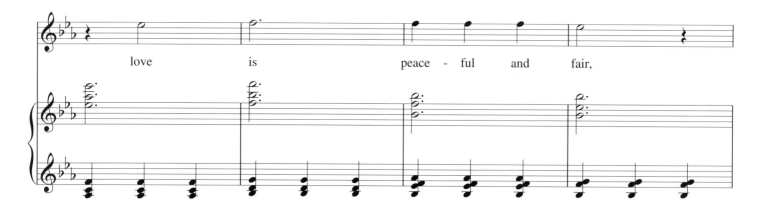

love   is   peace - ful   and   fair,

Love   can   creep   up   so   sud - den - ly;

poco rit.

when   you   least   think   of   it,   your   love   is   there.   We

colla voce   *a tempo*

all   want   a   world   filled   with   peace   and   with   joy,   with   plen - ty   of

f

A LITTLE BIT IN LOVE
from *Wonderful Town*

Lyrics by BETTY COMDEN
and ADOLPH GREEN
Music by LEONARD BERNSTEIN

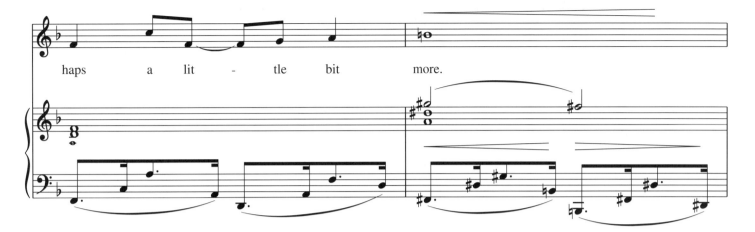

haps a lit - tle bit more.

(rhythmically)

When he ___ looks at me, ___ ev - 'ry-thing's ha - zy and all out of fo - cus.

When he ___ touch - es me, ___ I'm in the spell of a strange ho - cus po - cus.

It's so ___ I don't know. ___ I'm so ___ I don't know. ___ I don't

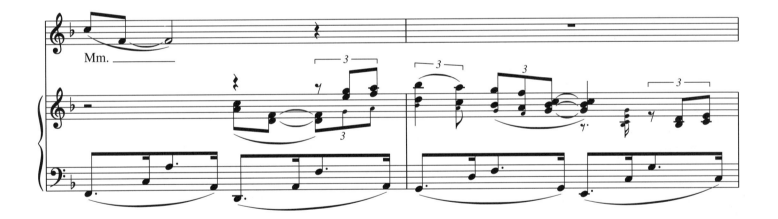

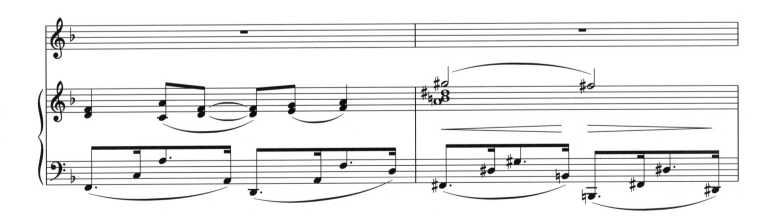

Mm, _____ It's so nice to be a-live ___ When you

meet some-one _____ who be-witch-es you. ___ Will he

be my all, ___ or did I just fall a lit-tle bit, ___ a

lit - tle bit in love. _____

WHY WAS I BORN?
from *Sweet Adeline*

Lyrics by OSCAR HAMMERSTEIN II
Music by JEROME KERN

Spend-ing these lone-some eve-nings With noth-ing to do but to live in dreams that I

make up, _____ All by my-self; _____

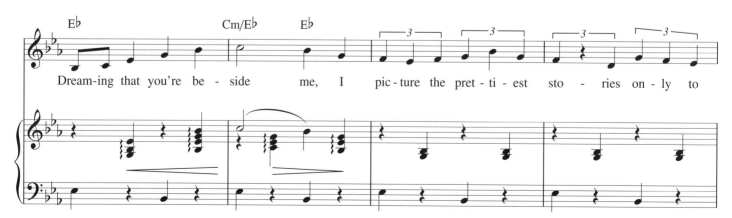

Dream-ing that you're be-side me, I pic-ture the pret-ti-est sto-ries on-ly to

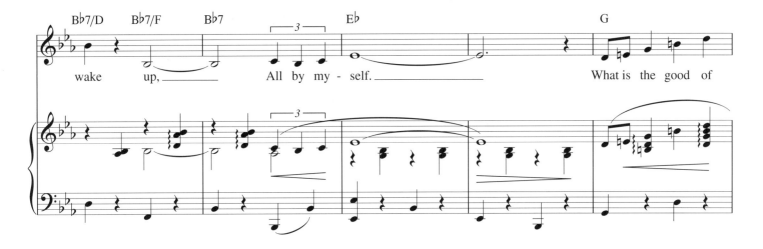

wake up,_____ All by my-self._____ What is the good of

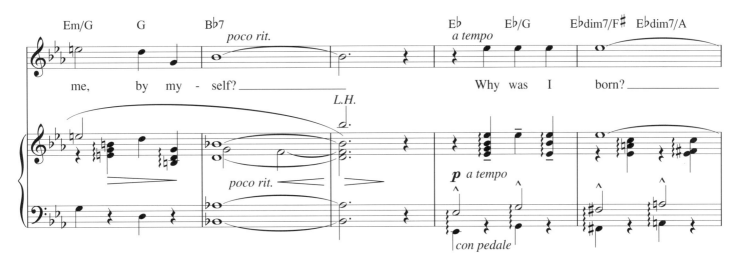

me, by my-self?_____ Why was I born?_____

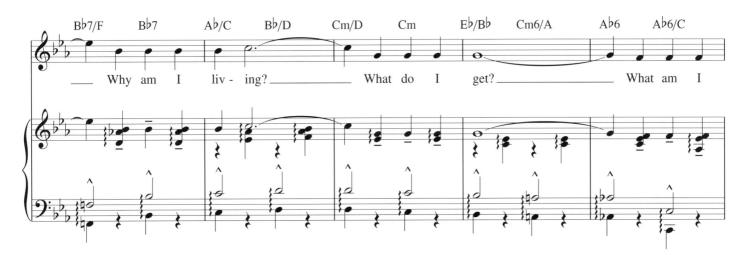

_____ Why am I liv-ing?_____ What do I get?_____ What am I

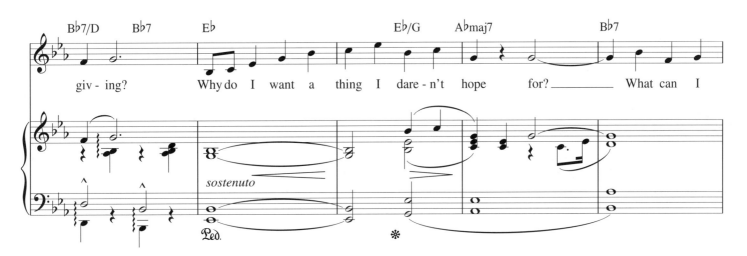

giv-ing? Why do I want a thing I dare-n't hope for?_____ What can I